C. Stangl

SHAKESPEARE

ROMEO AND JULIET IN EVERYDAY ENGLISH

COLES EDITORIAL BOARD

A NOTE TO THE READER

These Notes present a clear discussion of the action and thought of the work under consideration and a concise interpretation of its artistic merits and its significance.

They are intended as a supplementary aid to the serious student. They serve to free the student from interminable and distracting note-taking in class so that he may listen intelligently to what the instructor is saying, or to the class discussion, making selective notes on these, secure in the knowledge that he has the basic understanding. They are also helpful in preparing for an examination, saving not merely the burden but the confusion of trying to re-read the full text under pressure, and disentangling from a mass of—often illegible—notes that which is of central importance.

THE NOTES ARE NOT A SUBSTITUTE FOR THE TEXT ITSELF OR FOR THE CLASSROOM DISCUSSION OF THE TEXT, AND THE STUDENT WHO SO ATTEMPTS TO USE THEM IS DENYING HIMSELF THE VERY EDUCATION THAT HE IS PRESUMABLY GIVING HIS MOST VITAL YEARS TO ACHIEVE.

The critical evaluations have been prepared by experts with special knowledge of the individual texts who have usually had some years' experience in teaching the works. They are, however, not incontrovertible. No literary judgment is. Of any great work of literature there are many interpretations, and even conflicting views have value for the student (and the teacher), since the aim is not for the student to accept unquestioningly any one interpretation but to make his own.

COLES PUBLISHING COMPANY LIMITED
TORONTO — CANADA
PRINTED IN CANADA

CHARACTERS IN THE PLAY

Escalus: Prince of Verona.
Paris: A young nobleman; kinsman of Escalus.
Montague, **Capulet**: Heads of two houses; hostile to each other.
Lady Montague: Wife of Montague.
Lady Capulet: Wife of Capulet.
Romeo: Son of Montague.
Juliet: Daughter of Capulet.
Mercutio: Friend of Romeo; kinsman of Escalus.
Benvolio: Friend of Romeo; nephew of Montague.
Tybalt: Nephew of Lady Capulet.
Friar Laurence: A Franciscan.
Friar John: A Franciscan.
Balthasar: Romeo's servant.
Sampson, **Gregory**: Capulet's servants.
Nurse: Juliet's nurse.
Peter: Nurse's servant.
Abraham: Montague's servant.
Apothecary
Three Musicians
Citizens of Verona: Kinsmen and pages of both houses, maskers, guards, watchmen, attendants and chorus.

[*Setting: Verona; Mantua*.]

PROLOGUE

[Enter Chorus.]

Chorus: In the pleasant city of Verona dwelt two noble families. Between these two households there was a long-standing feud, which, at the time of our tale, had broken out again into open quarrel, and the hands of the rival followers of each household were stained with their fellow citizens' blood. Into these two unhappy households, torn by such a deadly quarrel, were born, respectively, a son and a daughter, who grew up to love each other dearly. But the heavens frowned upon their love, and fate fought against them. In the end, their sad misfortunes and unhappy death induced their parents to put an end to the feud that had led to so sorrowful a result.

The unhappy progress of their affection for each other, doomed by fate to lead only to their death, and the story of the ancient feud between their parents, a quarrel so fierce and deadly that nothing would, in any way, soften their hearts or move them to a reconciliation except the piteous end of their own son and daughter, is the tale that we set before you for an hour or two upon the stage. If, now, you will graciously listen to our tale, we shall, in our acting, endeavor to supply what may be missing in the written story.

ACT I · SCENE 1

[Verona, a public square.]

[Enter Sampson and Gregory, armed with swords and small shields.]

Sampson: I swear, Gregory, that we will not put up with insults. We will carry coals for no one!

Gregory: No indeed; only coal miners do that.

Sampson: What I would say is, that should anyone move us to anger, we will draw our swords upon them.

Gregory: Quite right. Always draw away from the prospect of bondage.

Sampson: I am very ready with a blow, when my feelings are stirred.

Gregory: But your feelings are not readily roused to the striking point.

Sampson: If it be anyone belonging to the household of

Montague, even a dog, that is sufficient to rouse me.

Gregory: But if you stir, you do not stand still. Now, brave men stand still in the presence of their foes, but you say you stir, therefore you must fly from them.

Sampson: The meanest thing belonging to Montague will make me fight. I will force any servant of his to walk outside the pavement, and give me the place next to the wall.

Gregory: Then you prove yourself weak, for it is the weak who are forced to the wall.

Sampson: I agree with you. That is the reason that women, who are not so strong as men, are always thrust aside. I will thrust Montague's servants out from the wall, and his maids toward it.

Gregory: But we have no quarrel with the maids, it is only our lords, and we, their men, who fight.

Sampson: I do not care for that, it is all the same to me. I will be harsh with all alike, and will fight with the men first and then turn my attention to the maids, and will take their heads.

Gregory: The maidens' heads?

Sampson: Yes, their maiden heads, or their maidenhood—if you like to take it in that sense.

Gregory: Well, those whom you set upon will know which it is, no doubt.

Sampson: I shall certainly stand up to them as long as I am able, and I think my character is pretty well-known by this time.

Gregory: Well, you are a man, at any rate. Out with your weapon, here are two of Montague's people approaching.

[*Enter Abraham and Balthasar.*]

Sampson: I have unsheathed my sword. You begin the quarrel, and I will back you up.

Gregory: Back me! Do you mean you will present your back to me, and run off?

Sampson: Do not be afraid!

Gregory: Afraid of you? No, indeed!

Sampson: Do not let us break the law, however, by forcing a quarrel. Let the other side commence it.

Gregory: I will glance at them in a surly manner as I pass, and they may be offended or not, as they choose.

Sampson: It will not be as they like, but as they dare. We will see if they dare take up the challenge or not. I will put my thumb to my mouth as we pass, which will insult them. They will be shamed before us if they do not resent it.

Abraham: Are you making that gesture at us, sir?

Sampson: I am making it, sir.

Abraham: Do you make it at us, sir?

Sampson: [*Aside to Gregory.*] If I say yes, are we within the law?

Gregory: No.

Sampson: No, sir, I do not make it at you, but I make it, sir.

Gregory: Do you wish to fight, sir?

Abraham: To fight? Not at all.

Sampson: If you do, I am ready. My master is as good a man as yours.

Abraham: But not a better one.

Sampson: All right, sir.

[*Enter Benvolio.*]

Gregory: [*Aside to Sampson.*] Say that our master is the better man, for I see a relation of his approaching.

Sampson: He is a better man, sir.

Abraham: That is false.

Sampson: Out with your swords, unless you are afraid. Gregory, forget not your swinging stroke.

[*They fight.*]

Benvolio: Stop, you foolish people! Separate at once. Sheathe your weapons, and show a little more wisdom.

[*Beats down their swords.*]

[*Enter Tybalt.*]

Tybalt: What, Benvolio! Do I find you with drawn sword among these cowardly rascals? Turn and face me, and be slain!

Benvolio: I am only trying to prevent this strife. Sheathe your weapon or only use it to help me separate these fellows.

Tybalt: Peace, indeed! When I find you with a naked sword in your hand? I detest the word "peace," as I detest Hades itself, and every kinsman of Montague, and yourself also. Fight, coward!

[*They fight.*]

[*Enter several of both households, who join the fight; then, enter citizens with clubs.*]

First Citizen: Come on! Bring your weapons, and overpower them. Down with every one, of both quarrelsome houses!

[*Enter Capulet, in his gown, and Lady Capulet.*]

Capulet: What is all this tumult? Bring me my weapon, someone!

Lady Capulet: You had better call for a staff to support you, rather than for a weapon to fight with.

Capulet: Bring me a weapon, I tell you! Here is Lord Montague, with his sword drawn in defiance of us.

[*Enter Montague and Lady Montague.*]

Montague: Capulet! You scoundrel! Let me come at him, hinder me not!

Lady Montague: Not one inch shall you move toward your enemy.

[*Enter prince with his followers.*]

Prince: O disobedient fools! You disturb the tranquillity of the city with your tumults, degrading your weapons by turning them against your fellow citizens. Do you refuse to listen to your prince?

Hear me, you men, who forget your humanity in raging upon each other like wolves, whose fierce fury will not be satisfied except by the blood of your foes. Cast down at once those swords, which you have turned in anger against your fellows, or look for severe punishment at my hands. Listen to the judgment of your angered ruler.

On three different occasions have you, Lord Montague and Lord Capulet, broken the peace of the city by your brawls, arising out of a mere breath, the faintest of excuses. You have caused aged citizens and sober townspeople, laying aside their more customary habits and adornments, to take to their weapons once more, grasping their ancient pikes in aged hands withered by long disuse, to separate your riotous followers, whose habitual hatred breaks out in these constant tumults. On the very next occurrence of such a disturbance, death shall be the penalty dealt out to all. I dismiss your followers on this occasion only, but you, Lord Capulet, must accompany me. This afternoon, Lord Montague, I shall expect you at the place of judgment, and shall there tell you my will in this matter. Again I say, disperse quickly, or forfeit your lives.

[*Exit all but Montague, Lady Montague and Benvolio.*]

Montague: Whose fault was it that this old strife has been renewed? Tell us of the matter, kinsman. Were you present when the disturbance commenced?

Benvolio: The followers of your enemy, and your own, had already met and were hotly engaged when I arrived upon the scene. I unsheathed my sword and tried to separate them and, at that moment, the hot-tempered Tybalt appeared, with his sword already drawn. Swiftly challenging me, he swung his weapon aloft, cleaving only the air, which whistled disdainfully around his head. Then, as we engaged each other in fighting, a number of people joined the fray and took part with one side or the other, until the prince appeared and compelled the two sides to separate.

Lady Montague: Have you seen my son today? Do you know where he is? I am most thankful that he was absent from this fight.

Benvolio: Lady, my sad thoughts did, this morning, impel me to seek the open air, sometime before dawn, when the glorious sun, the adoration of so many multitudes, had not yet looked forth with brilliant gaze from out of the shining east. There, under the shade of the plane trees which grow westward from the city walls, I saw Romeo walking at that early hour. I went toward him, but he noticed my approach and quickly hid himself amid the trees. Judging the state of his feelings by my own, I felt that he was fully occupied by his own thoughts, and I avoided him willingly, as this suited my humor as well as his, and pleased us both equally well.

Montague: Day after day, he has been found there at that early hour, adding his teardrops to the watery dews of dawn, and breathing forth cloudy sighs to join the cloudy skies. However, no sooner does the sun with gladdening rays begin to chase away the shades of night, and drive apart the veil that hides the rosy morning, than sad-hearted Romeo turns his steps homeward and flees from its golden splendor. He goes to his room, and locking his chamber door, darkens the room, excluding the bright sun, and there he sits alone, in gloom. I greatly fear that this state of mind will destroy his health, unless someone with wisdom enough to understand the case can give us good advice, and remove the reason for his sadness.

Benvolio: Do you know the reason, my lord?

Montague: I do not, nor can I find it out from Romeo.

Benvolio: Have you ever inquired it of him?

Montague: Both myself and many of our acquaintances have asked him frequently, but he keeps his feelings to himself, and is, as far as regards his state of mind, I cannot exactly say faithful, for I do not know, but is so secret and reserved, and so impenetrable to any probings or searchings that he resembles a rosebud at the root of which a caterpillar is gnawing, so that it can never open out its perfumed petals, or offer its full-blown loveliness to the view of the god of day. We should rejoice, equally, to know the reason for his sadness, and to apply a remedy.

[*Enter Romeo.*]

Benvolio: Look! Romeo is approaching. If you will now be good enough to leave us together, I shall learn the cause of his grief, unless he is very steadfast in his refusal to reveal it.

Montague: I only hope you will be fortunate enough to make him tell you the real cause. Let us go, lady.

[*Exit Montague and Lady Montague.*]

Benvolio: Good morning, kinsman.

Romeo: Is it still morning?

Benvolio: The hour of nine has only just chimed.

Romeo: Alas! How slowly time passes when one is sorrowful! Was that my father who hurried away just now?

Benvolio: Yes. What sorrow is it that makes your hours seem long?

Romeo: The lack of something which would, if I possessed it, make them fly all too quickly.

Benvolio: Are you in love?

Romeo: Not—

Benvolio: In love?

Romeo: Not in the good graces of the lady whom I love.

Benvolio: Ah, me! How sad that love, so attractive and mild in appearance, should, so often, prove stern and oppressive in experience!

Romeo: Ah, me! How sad that love, so often called blind, should yet, despite his blindness, find his way to smite what hearts he will!

Where shall we go and take a meal together? What a fight there has been here! You need not, however, describe it to me, for I know all about it. It arose from hatred, and yet love is connected with it, too. O love, which leads to brawls and strife! Which even breeds hate, because of those we love! It is a nameless feeling, bred of nothing tangible, which weighs upon the spirits, yet also makes them buoyant, a fruitless, unsatisfying quest, yet followed with ardor and sincerity, a confused dream of beauty, a leaden-weighted lightness, a freezing heat, a shining cloud, a vigorous weakness, a mass of contradictions and a state in which the body is active, while the mind is lost in dreamland! Such are my feelings of affection, but I confess I have no affection for such feelings! Are you not moved to laughter?

Benvolio: No, cousin. Rather, to tears.

Romeo: Kind-hearted cousin, for what are your tears?

Benvolio: For the burden, which your kind heart is bearing.

Romeo: Such a burden is the penalty of love. If you grieve for me, you add to the sorrow, which already weighs me down. The loving sympathy, which you have manifested toward me only multiplies my sadness, in seeing you grieve. Love is a breath, a vapor, made of lovers' sighs. When pure, it is a flame which lightens lovers' eyes, when crossed and troubled, an ocean fed by lovers' tears, and what is it besides? A wise insanity, a sober frenzy, a bitterness which kills and a life-giving delight. Adieu, cousin.

[*Going.*]

Benvolio: Wait a moment, I will accompany you. You are unkind if you leave me like this.

Romeo: It is not I, who would treat you so. I am not myself at present.

Benvolio: Now, without any jesting, tell me the lady's name.

Romeo: Must I look sorrowful to do it?

Benvolio: Not at all. But tell me in sober truth.

Romeo: I am as reluctant to do it, as a sick man is to make his will. It seems to me an ill-timed and annoying request. However, in sober truth, it is a woman whom I love!

Benvolio: I supposed as much, when I guessed you were in love.

Romeo: You hit the mark well! And the lady whom I love is beautiful!

Benvolio: And a beautiful woman is a mark well seen and most often aimed at.

Romeo: You have missed your aim this time, for the lady

refuses to be pierced by the shafts of the god of Love. She is of the same mind as the virgin Huntress, and, secure in her armor of chastity, she lives untouched by the puny efforts of Cupid to attack her. She will not allow her heart to be taken by storm, either by winning speeches or pleading glances. Nor will she yield to the charms of wealth, though saints might be tempted by it to forsake the paths of virtue. Of beauty, she has great store, and her only poverty is her inability to leave that wealth behind her when she dies.

Benvolio: Has she then vowed that she will never wed?

Romeo: Yes, and in vowing to be so miserly with her charms, she is guilty of great wastefulness, throwing away her beauty without perpetuating it. Vows like hers, kept with such strictness, would entirely deprive future ages of all beauty. She has so much wisdom, and so much beauty, that surely she will not keep to her resolve, and leave me without hope in the end! Yet she has resolved to renounce love, and, for that reason, though I still live, I am dead to all that makes life of any worth.

Benvolio: Let me advise you. Try to banish her from your mind.

Romeo: How can I banish her from my mind, when she occupies my every thought?

Benvolio: By ceasing to fix your eyes on her alone. Let your glances rest on other fair ladies.

Romeo: That would only result in my finding her beauty more transcendent, the more I examined and compared. The very blackness of those masks, fortunate in being allowed to touch the lovely faces they hide, only serves to emphasize the beauty we know they conceal. To lose one's eyesight would only emphasize the remembrance of the beauty one could no longer see. And to ask me to look upon other lovely faces could have no other result than to bring more forcibly to my mind that face which was lovelier than all. Adieu! Your efforts are useless. I must remember still!

Benvolio: I will teach you, should it take all my life!

[*Exit.*]

ACT I · SCENE 2

[*Enter Capulet, Paris and servant.*]

Capulet: Both Montague and myself are under the same sentence, and are both under a promise to refrain from any further disturbance, which should not be difficult for either of us, at our age.

Paris: You are both held in high esteem, and it is a matter for great regret that the quarrel has lasted so long between you. And now, sir, what is your answer to my request?

Capulet: I can say no more than I have already said. My daughter is still very young, and knows nothing of the world, for she is scarcely yet 14. Wait awhile. We ought not to think of her possible marriage for at least another two years.

Paris: Maidens of tenderer age than Juliet are often happily wedded.

Capulet: And those who are so wedded, at that early age, too soon lose all their beauty. All my children, excepting this one, are laid to rest in the earth. She is my only hope, the sole remaining one. Court her, however, and gain her affections if you will. Her consent is the first necessity, and my agreement thereto is merely secondary. If she is willing, my assent and concurrence lie in the same direction. It is my custom to give a banquet on this night of the year, and many of my dearest friends and those whom I most respect will be present. Your most welcome presence, added to the rest, will give me great pleasure.

This evening, at my humble abode, you may expect to see maidens of such starry radiance, as will light up this dull earth and make the darkened skies of little account. You may enjoy such pleasure among the sweet, opening flowers of womanhood as vigorous young manhood always inclines to do, when the long lingering winter is chased away by beauteous spring in all its fresh array. Come and look at all there is to see and hear, and then fix your regard on the one who shall appear most worthy of it. My daughter may, although seen among so many fair faces, still be the one you approve, although she is but one. Will you accompany me?

[*To servant, giving a paper.*] Here, fellow, take this paper, and hasten through the town to those whose names I have written down, and say that I wait to welcome them to my dwelling.

[*Exit Capulet and Paris.*]

Servant: I am to seek out those in this list! The proverb says that a cobbler should stick to his measure, and the maker of clothes to his last, the fisherman busy himself with his pencil, and the artist with his nets, and so each one to his own trade. Here am I, who never learned to read, set to find out what writing is here set down. I must go to someone wiser than myself. And, in a lucky moment, here is someone approaching.

[*Enter Benvolio and Romeo.*]

Benvolio: Nay, then, you may take out the sting of a burn by applying other heat to it, and one pain may be forgotten, on the occurrence of a second pain. When one is giddy, the best cure is to reverse the direction in which one has turned, and the misery of a fresh sorrow will drive out the grief which occupied us before. Only expose yourself to a fresh attack, and the severity of the old fever will wear itself out.

Romeo: Plantain leaves are excellent in that case.

Benvolio: In what case, pray?

Romeo: For a bruised shin.

Benvolio: Have you taken leave of your senses?

Romeo: No, though I experience the same treatment. My fetters are stronger than a madman's are. I am starved and imprisoned, scourged and tortured, and—good evening, my man.

Servant: God be with you, sir. Tell me, sir, whether you can read.

Romeo: Yes, I can read my own unhappy fortune.

Servant: You may have learned that without its being written down, but tell me, sir, can you read whatever is set before you?

Romeo: Yes, if it be written in language that I can understand.

Servant: No doubt, sir, that is true. Joy be with you!

Romeo: Stop, man. I know how to read. [*Reads.*] "Signior Martino and his wife and daughters; Count Anselm and his lovely sisters; the lady widow of Vitruvio; Signior Placentio and his fair nieces; Mercutio and his brother, Valentine; my uncle Capulet and his wife and daughters; my pretty niece Rosaline; Livia; Signior Valentio and his cousin Tybalt; Lucio and the sprightly Helena."

A noble company! Where are they to come?

Servant: Up.

Romeo: Where to?

Servant: To where we live. They are asked to supper.
Romeo: At whose house?
Servant: At my lord's house.
Romeo: Ah, I ought first to have inquired who he is.
Servant: I will inform you, now, before you ask. My lord is the wealthy Lord Capulet, and, unless you belong to Montague's household, you are welcome to come and drink with the rest. Good luck sir!

[*Exit.*]

Benvolio: The lovely Rosaline, upon whom your affections are so set, is to be at this time-honored feast in Capulet's house, in company with all the fairest ladies in the city. Come to that feast, and impartially judge her in comparison with others whom I shall point out, and you shall own that she, whom you think so lovely, is less fair than she seemed.
Romeo: Never, until tears change to fires, will my eyes, which worship her, admit such a heresy, and those same eyes which, though often drenched with weeping, yet could never die, should die the death of heretics, and perish by fire. Show me one more beauteous than my lady! Never, since the beginning of time, has the sun's glance rested on her equal.
Benvolio: Nonsense! She looked beautiful in your eyes because you looked at her alone, and there was no one else with whom you could compare her. Balance her beauty in your eyes against that of one, whom I shall point out to you at the banquet tonight, whose beauty is radiant as a star, and you shall acknowledge that she, whom you now place above all others, is scarcely worthy of a place among the many fair ones we shall see.
Romeo: I will accompany you—not to see others fairer, as you promise, but to delight my heart by proving my own lady fairest of all.

[*Exit.*]

ACT I · SCENE 3

[*A room in Capulet's house.*]
[*Enter Lady Capulet and Nurse.*]

Lady Capulet: Bring my little girl to me, Nurse. Where is she?
Nurse: I have already told her. Come, little one! Where are you, my bird? Juliet!

[*Enter Juliet.*]

Juliet: What is all this? Who wants me?

Nurse: Your mother.

Juliet: I am at your service, lady. What do you wish?

Lady Capulet: I wish to speak to you on a certain matter. Nurse, leave us for a time, I wish to speak to my daughter alone. No! You may remain. Now that I consider the matter, you may hear what I have to say. You know that Juliet is now growing up.

Nurse: Indeed, I can tell exactly how old she is.

Lady Capulet: She is scarcely 14 years of age.

Nurse: I will wager 14 of my teeth—only, to my sorrow, four are all I possess—that you are right. How long will it be before the first day of August arrives?

Lady Capulet: Two weeks and a few odd days.

Nurse: Odd or not, that is the very day she was born. It will be 14 years on the night before August 1st since she was born. My own daughter, Susan, was born at the same time—peace be with her soul! I was not worthy to keep her, and she is now in Paradise. Well, as I have told you, Juliet will be 14 years of age on the night before Lammas Day, indeed she will. I do not forget.

She was taken from the breast on the day of the earthquake, and that is 11 years ago. I was sitting by the pigeon shelter, and had put a bitter herb on my breast. You, my lady, were absent at the time, being with Lord Capulet at Mantua (what a memory I have!). As I was saying, I had touched my breast with a bitter herb, and when the dear little innocent felt the bitter taste, it was amusing to see how angry she was, and how she quarrelled with the teat! The pigeon shelter shook, and I was needed no more after that to give the little one milk.

That is 11 years ago. She was able to stand and to toddle alone then, I swear, for she had fallen and bruised her forehead only the day before. My husband—peace to his soul, he always loved a jest—picked the little one up, and said to her, "Well, well! Have you fallen on your forehead? When you know better, you will fall the other way, will you not, little maid!" and, upon my word, the sweet babe stopped its weeping, and said, "Yes." Only think of it, after all these years! I shall never forget it, no matter to what age I may live. "Won't you, little maid?" cried he and the lovely little innocent stopped crying, and answered, "Yes."

Lady Capulet: That will do, Nurse. Say no more, I beg you.

Nurse: Very well, lady. Still, I cannot help laughing when I remember how the child stopped weeping and said, "Yes," although, really, it was a dangerous blow, and there was quite a large bump on her forehead, and she was weeping heavily. But my husband said, "Did you fall on your face, little one? You will fall the other way when you are older, will you?" And she stopped and answered, "Yes."

Juliet: I wish you would stop too, Nurse!

Nurse: I will say not another word. Heaven bless you! If I only live long enough to see you wedded, I shall have had my heart's desire.

Lady Capulet: And that is the very subject I came to discuss. What do you think, my daughter, of being married?

Juliet: I have never yet had the slightest idea of being married.

Nurse: No idea of it! I would say that she must have drunk in wisdom with her childhood's milk, except that I should then be praising myself.

Lady Capulet: Let your mind dwell upon the subject now, my daughter. Ladies of even less than your age in this city are already married. Indeed, if I calculate rightly, you were born when I was not much more than your age. To come to the point, then, the brave young Paris is a suitor for your hand.

Nurse: A gallant young gentleman! A youth such as anyone might—why, he is a most handsome man.

Lady Capulet: There is not another so handsome in all Verona.

Nurse: Indeed, he is the best, the very best.

Lady Capulet: What think you, Juliet? Will it be possible for you to love him? You will see him this evening, at the banquet in our house. Observe then the beauty of his countenance, note well how one fair feature enhances the grace of another, and how all harmonize with each other, and whatever is not revealed by his features, look for in the luster of his eyes. He is like a costly volume of worthy contents, only needing a beautiful binding to make it worthier still. As the fish's glittering scales are set off by the water in which it moves, so it is fitting that a beautiful interior should be adorned by a fair outside. In the opinion of many people, a costly binding adds to the worth of a volume's contents, which share in the honor, which so fine an outside bestows. In the same way, will your charms and wealth be enhanced by his, when you are united to him, and his graces shall make yours more complete.

Nurse: Quite right! You are certainly not exaggerating the advantages of marriage.

Lady Capulet: Now say, in a word, whether you think you can look favorably on his courtship.

Juliet: I will observe him with that intention, if observation will lead to that end. But I shall not commit myself any farther than to look because you wish me to do so.

[*Enter a servant.*]

Servant: Lady, your visitors have arrived, and the feast is spread. You and the young lady are inquired for, and the servants are screaming at Nurse for her absence from the pantry. The bustle is at its height, and I must go at once to serve the guests. Come quickly, I beg of you.

Lady Capulet: We are coming. [*Exit servant.*] Count Paris waits for you, my daughter.

Nurse: Go, my love, and find joy awaiting you.

[*Exit.*]

ACT I · SCENE 4

[*A street.*]

[*Enter Romeo, Mercutio and Benvolio with five or six masqueraders, torchbearers and others.*]

Romeo: Well, shall we enter and join in the revels without explanation, or would it be better to give the customary speech?

Benvolio: Oh! These long-winded orations are quite old-fashioned now. We will have none of these devices of concealment, entering like a Cupid with bandaged eyes and imitation bow, fantastically attired, like scarecrows, frightening the guests. Neither will we go in with stammering apologies, hesitatingly delivered, with much prompting, to mark our arrival. They may judge us as they will. We shall only remain to join in the dance awhile, and then depart.

Romeo: I shall not dance. Let me be a torchbearer, as I am heavy-hearted just now, it will suit me best to hold a light.

Mercutio: Not at all, my dear Romeo, you must join the dancers.

Romeo: Indeed, no. You are light-hearted and light-footed, but the heaviness of my spirits weighs me to the earth, and keeps me from the dance.

Mercutio: Are you not in love? Your spirits should, with Cupid's aid, be able to rise higher than those of ordinary mortals.

Romeo: Cupid's arrow has wounded me too deeply for me to be able to fly with his wings. I cannot leap out of my misery, my load is too heavy.

Mercutio: And you are too heavy a weight for love to sustain. It is too delicate.

Romeo: Is love gentle? I have not found it so. It is fierce, harsh and stormy, and pierces sharply.

Mercutio: Then render love back its own treatment. Be harsh and severe with it, and you will conquer it. Come, give me a visor to put over my face—[*putting on a mask*]— a mask to cover a mask! I care nothing for all the inquisitive glances that may be cast at me to observe my looks. This mask above my eyes will do all the blushing I require.

Benvolio: Come, let us go in now, and, as soon as we enter, let all join in the dance.

Romeo: I'll be a torchbearer. The frolicsome revellers may stir the rushes with nimble feet, but I am inclined to follow the ancient proverb, and be the onlooker who holds the candle. I never cared for the game, in any case, and I shall dance no more.

Mercutio: Nonsense, man! Dull is the mouse, as the constable says, but if you are dull, we'll play the game of drawing you out of the mud of such objectionable love as you are buried in. Come along, we are wasting lights by daytime.

Romeo: Nay, that cannot be.

Mercutio: I mean that we are wasting our time as uselessly as we would be wasting candles, if we lighted them in daylight. You must look for the idea contained in my words, and not take them literally, for you will find my meaning, many times in the figurative sense, for once, in the literal interpretation.

Romeo: And insofar as the idea goes, it is a good thing to be going to this entertainment. But, literally, it is most unwise to do so.

Mercutio: Might I inquire your reason?

Romeo: Because of a dream I have had.

Mercutio: I had one also.

Romeo: What did you dream?

Mercutio: That dreamers often lie.

Romeo: Yes, lie on their couches, where in their slumbers, they often have true visions.

Mercutio: Ah! You have had a visit from the Fairy Queen. I see. She visits dreamers as they lie slumbering, and brings forth their fancies into shape, making them take seeming form and reality. A tiny visitant she is, no larger than a cameo on a mayor's ring and, as the slumberers lie on their beds, she drives across their faces, drawn by tiny creatures, in a fairy chariot, under a canopy of grasshoppers' wings. The spokes of the chariot wheels are of the crane-fly's long and delicate legs, and the finest gossamer threads form the harness. Sparkling moonbeams are the arching collars of the steeds, a gossamer thread forms her whip, and the handle is a tiny insect's bone, and her charioteer, all dressed in gray, a little gnat, smaller than the smallest worm supposed to find its home in the fingers of slothful maids. The fairy coach he drives is fashioned of an empty nutshell, and built by Master Squirrel, a skilful carpenter, or by Master Caterpillar, for these two, from time immemorial, have made the chariots, which the fairies use.

Thus equipped, Queen Mab takes her nightly journeys. Sometimes, she drives across a lover's brain, and immediately he sees a vision of his lady. Sometimes, it is a courtier's knees she crosses, and then he fancies he is at the court making obeisance to the great ones there. Again, a lawyer's hand feels her light touch and, in his dreams, he is receiving money. Sometimes, she brushes over the lips of ladies, and then they think their lovers kiss them on the mouth. But now and then, she finds that the maidens have been indulging in too many delicacies and, in her displeasure, she punishes the fair ones with blistered lips. Then, she drives over the face of one who haunts the courts, and he dreams that he is following up some plan for his own advancement. Over the face of a priest she comes and, arousing memories of tithe payments, he dreams that a richer living is presented to him.

To the warrior she comes also, and gallops across his neck. Then, he sees visions of wars, in which he slays enemies, takes part in sieges and breaks down a city's walls, is in peril from a foe in ambush, and from the swords of his enemies. After, he is carousing with his comrades, and drinking deep draughts of wine. Then, suddenly, the mischievous fairy sounds a loud alarm close to his ear, and he springs up from sleep. Then, recovering from his alarm, mutters mingled oaths and prayers, and sinks down to slumber once more.

It is the same tricky fairy that twists the horses' manes into knots, and mats together the hair of uncleanly persons, and it is supposed to foretell great ill luck if this be interfered with. It is this fairy who—

Romeo: Stop! Stop! My friend, say no more, your words are but idle air.

Mercutio: You are right, I was speaking of visionary themes, unsubstantial fancies, the outcome of imagination alone, which is as light and intangible as the air we breathe, and more variable than the breezes that, one moment, courts the icy northern plains, then, suddenly in displeasure, blows in fierce gusts away, and seeks the moist and balmy fields of southern lands.

Benvolio: Well, these breezes you are discussing are keeping us from our own affairs. The banquet will be over before we get there.

Romeo: I feel that, even now, we shall enter too soon, for my heart is full of dread. I see foreshadowed some event not yet disclosed, the outcome of our present acts. Later, we shall be able to trace all the misfortunes which follow, to the night on which we joined in these festivities. Some dread event will surely end my life, and still the heart that beats in this bosom, by some hateful means, which yet I know not of, and will bring me, all too early, to a miserable end. However, let the Power that guides my life and arranges my fate pilot me along the appointed road. Forward, good fellows.

Benvolio: Drummer, begin!

[*Exit.*]

ACT I · SCENE 5

[*A large room in Capulet's house. Musicians waiting. Enter servants.*]

First Servant: What has become of Potpan, that he is not here to help us to clear away after the feast? Trust him to be absent, when he ought to be helping to carry away the plates!

Second Servant: Things have come to a pretty pass, when only one or two remember their duty and use their hands as they ought—and those hands dirty, too!

First Servant: Fold up the seats, and carry them off. Take away the sideboard, and see that the silver is all right. And do, my good fellow, keep a piece of sweet cake for me, and beg the porter to allow Susan Grindstone and Nell to come in, for my sake. Antony! Potpan!

Second Servant: Yes, here I am, ready!

First Servant: You are wanted, and required, and waited for in the big hall.

Third Servant: It is impossible for us to be in two places at once. Hurry up happily, comrades, work hard for awhile, those who live longest will get most.

[*They retire behind.*]

[*Enter Capulet with Juliet and others of his house, meeting the guests and masqueraders.*]

Capulet: Greetings, sirs! Here you will find partners willing to dance with you, unless they are troubled with corns. Now, my fair ladies, which of you will dare refuse to dance after that! If any of you hold back now, I shall declare it is because you have corns. Ah! Does that touch you? Welcome once more, sirs. I myself, at one time, could wear a mask, and join in the dance, and breathe sweet words in my partner's ear! Alas! Those days are over, but I rejoice to see you all here, gentlemen. Let the music begin, and give us room. Make room, and dance, ladies all.

[*Music plays, and they dance.*]

Bring more torches, fellows! Set the tables up against the walls and put out the fire, the hall grows too warm. Ah! My friend, this is delightful, this unexpected gaiety. Let us seat ourselves, good kinsman, for we two are grown too old to join in the dance. How many years have passed, since we last took in a masque?

Second Capulet: In faith, it must be 30 years ago.

Capulet: Nonsense, it is not so long as that! No matter how soon Whitsuntide may arrive, it will only be 25 years, then, since our friend Lucentio was married, and you and I wore masks at his wedding feast.

Second Capulet: It is more than that, sir, for Lucentio's son is 30 years of age.

Capulet: Do you indeed say so? It is but a year or two since his son was a minor.

Romeo: Who is that maiden who honors yon knight by giving him her hand?

Servant: I cannot tell you, sir.

Romeo: The radiance of her beauty shames the poor flame of the torches. She glows in the darkness of night like a lustrous gem adorning the dusky head of an Ethiopian. Hers is a loveliness too precious for daily sight, too rare for this dull world. She shines amid her companions as would a pure white dove consorting with crows. I shall notice where she takes up her position when this dance is over, and I shall venture to ask her to grace my rough hand, by allowing me to touch hers. Can I believe that I was ever in love before this! Let my eyes swear that it is false, and that they have never looked upon true loveliness till now!

Tybalt: That is the voice of a Montague! Fellow, bring me my sword. How dare the villain enter this house and under the mask of revelry, sneer at our doings, and hold our feast day up to contempt! I swear by the honor of my kinsfolk, and of the house to which I belong, I shall think it no crime to slay him on the spot.

Capulet: What is the matter, cousin? Why are you so angry?

Tybalt: A Montague is here, my lord. There he is, the enemy of our house, come with no good intention, but only to mock at our ceremony.

Capulet: Is it the youth, Romeo?

Tybalt: Yes, that is the scoundrel.

Capulet: Calm yourself, nephew, and do not meddle with him. His behavior is dignified and gentlemanly, and I have heard that all the town speaks well of him, saying that he is an excellent youth, and of well-regulated conduct. I would not have him insulted in my house for all the riches of Verona. So calm yourself, and leave him alone. I command you to do so, and if you have any regard for my wishes, clear away that angry look from your countenance, and show a more cheerful face. Such dark looks are most unsuitable for an occasion such as this.

Tybalt: They are very suitable, when a scoundrel such as Romeo is present. I will not tolerate it!

Capulet: He shall be tolerated. Indeed, my young friend, I will not have him molested. Is it your place to command in this house, or mine? *You*, indeed, will not put up with him! In Heaven's name, is it you that will raise a tumult among my visitors? You will set every one by the ears, will you? A pretty fellow!

Tybalt: It is a disgrace to us to endure his presence.

Capulet: Nonsense! That will do! You are an insolent young fellow. Really, do you say so? This notion of yours may cost you dear, I know in what way. You, indeed! To presume to cross my will! You say truly, good friends! Get you gone, you young coxcomb, and calm yourself, or light up more torches! You ought to be ashamed of yourself! I insist on your making no disturbance. Be merry, friends.

Tybalt: My passionate anger, warring with the restraint you force upon me, stirs me too profoundly to allow of my remaining here. I shall go, but Romeo shall dearly pay for forcing his presence upon us, and the present pleasure he enjoys shall cost him bitter pain.

[*Exit.*]

Romeo: [*To Juliet.*] If it be desecration for my hand to touch so sacred a temple of beauty, I am ready to make amends. My lips shall atone for my fingers' rudeness, as pilgrims approach and kiss the shrine of their divinity.

Juliet: Holy palmer, your hands are not deserving of such discredit, they only appear courteously reverent. A pilgrim's hand may, without rebuke, touch that of a saint, and to lay hand in hand is the usual greeting of pilgrims.

Romeo: If pilgrim and saint may lay hand to hand, may they do so with lips also?

Juliet: Their lips, pilgrim, are to be used for prayers.

Romeo: Ah! Dear saint, will you not allow lips to greet, as well as hands? Let my lips present the petition, and do yours grant it, for prayers ungranted make men's faith waver and die.

Juliet: Saints must not swerve from right, though they may grant a petition.

Romeo: Then do not swerve while I take the answer to my petition. So your lips have from mine taken away the guilt. [*Kissing her.*]

Juliet: It follows, then, that the guilt is now upon my lips, if they have taken it from yours.

Romeo: Taken guilt from me? Oh, how sweetly sounds such an accusation! Then give it back to me.

Juliet: You give and take your kisses by rule.

Nurse: Your mother begs you, lady, to come and speak with her.

Romeo: Who is the lady's mother?

Nurse: Young man, her mother is your hostess, and an excellent lady, and her daughter, to whom you were speaking, was nursed by me. Mark my words, he who succeeds in getting that young lady will gain much wealth.

Romeo: Does she belong to the house of Capulet? Oh, news that shall cost me dear! Now my very existence depends on one who is my enemy.

Benvolio: Come, let us take our leave. We shall not see anything better by staying longer.

Romeo: Indeed, I fear that is true, and I am the more sad because of it.

Capulet: Good friends, do not yet make preparations for departing, there is some small refreshment still to come. Will you really go? If you must do so, then thanks for your company. Many thanks, worthy friends. Good night. Bring more light this way! Now, let us go to our rest. Yes, indeed, the hour grows late. I will seek my chamber.

[*Exit all but Juliet and Nurse.*]

Juliet: Nurse, come here. Who is yonder youth?

Nurse: That is the aged Tiberio's son, and his heir.

Juliet: Who is that one just leaving the door?

Nurse: I believe that is young Petruchio.

Juliet: And who is the one behind him—the one who did not join in the dancing?

Nurse: I cannot tell.

Juliet: Go and inquire what his name is. If he should prove to be already married, my tomb will be the only wedding chamber I am likely to know.

Nurse: He is called Romeo, and he is the only son of Montague, the greatest enemy of your house.

Juliet: To think that I have fallen in love with one whom I am bound to hate! Alas! I saw him too soon, before knowing who he was, and now that I know, it is too late to recall my love. Love has brought me a doubtful gift, seeing that I have given my heart to my deadliest foe!

Nurse: What are you saying?

Juliet: Only some verses I learned from one of my partners in the dance.

[*A call within, "Juliet!"*]

Nurse: Coming! Coming! Let us go; all the guests have departed.

[*Exit.*]

ACT II · PROLOGUE

[*Enter Chorus.*]

Chorus: Now in Romeo's heart, his former fancy for Rosaline is almost dead, and a new and truer love impatiently longs to fill his whole being, in succession to that earlier desire. The maid whom he thought so beautiful, and for whom he thought he would die, is now seen to be far from the beauteous being he had pictured her, when compared with the fresh young loveliness of Capulet's daughter.

The youth and the maiden, each charmed by the other's beauty, are now deeply in love with each other. But the youth's tale of love must be poured forth to one whom he ought to regard as an enemy, and she must run risks and brave perils in order to taste the pleasures of his love.

He is denied all the usual privileges of a lover, being regarded as an enemy by her kinsfolk and, thus, he may not openly seek his lady's presence. While she, who loves equally dearly, has even fewer means of making opportunities of meeting the lover who is so dear to her. But the ardor of their affection devises ways and occasions of meeting, and the sweet delight they feel in each other's love enables them to make light of the perils they encounter and the risks they run.

ACT II · SCENE 1

[*Verona. A lane by the wall of Capulet's orchard.*]

[*Enter Romeo.*]

Romeo: How can I leave this place when the very core of my being remains here! Gross earthly flesh, return and seek thy heart, the pivot on which thy life revolves!

[*He climbs the wall, and leaps down within it.*]

[*Enter Benvolio and Mercutio.*]

Benvolio: Romeo! My friend Romeo!

Mercutio: He is not so foolish as we are. I dare swear he has slipped away home to rest.

Benvolio: I saw him come in this direction, and vault over the wall of the garden. See if you can make him hear, friend Mercutio.

Mercutio: I will not merely call him, I will invoke his presence by all the charms which I can think of that will work upon him. Romeo! Man of moods! Maniac! Ardent one! Lover! Show your presence! Come before us in the guise of a sigh, or let us hear only a single verse of poetry, and it will be proof sufficient that a lover is here! Only exclaim "Alas!" Or seek to match rhymes with "love." Address one flattering title to the Queen of Love, or find another name for the little blind Cupid, her son, who so excellently hit his mark when his shaft pierced the heart of King Cophetua, and filled it with love for the beggar maid.

Not a sound! Not a word, or movement! The poor young fellow is dead. I must invoke his spirit. By the shining eyes of Rosaline, by her beautiful features and shapely limbs, I conjure thee to appear before us in thine own proper form!

Benvolio: He will be much annoyed, if he can hear what you say.

Mercutio: Why should he be annoyed by what I have said? I have not invoked some stranger, but only called himself up by the use of Rosaline's name, using the most potent spell I could think of for Romeo himself.

Benvolio: We shall find that he is concealing himself purposely among the trees. His moods and fancies suit the dews and damps of night, for he is blinded by passion, and therefore the absence of light makes no difference to him.

Mercutio: If men are blinded by affection, then they will miss their aim. Now Romeo will seat himself under the boughs, and think upon his mistress. Good night, sir lover, the couch you choose in the open air is not warm enough for my comfort. I will go to my own little couch! Come, friends, shall we leave him?

Benvolio: Yes, let us go. It is useless to search for one who is deliberately hiding himself.

[*Exit.*]

ACT II · SCENE 2

[*Capulet's orchard.*]

[*Enter Romeo.*]

Romeo: Those who mock at the wounds which love deals, are those who have never experienced the smart of them.

[*Juliet appears above at a window.*]

But see! What bright beams shine from that window

above me? That window is the point from which the daybreak springs and the sun which rises there is Capulet's fair daughter! Shine out, radiant sun, and eclipse the pale and sickly moon, which now grows sad and dim, to see a virgin follower of hers so much fairer than herself. Cast off your allegiance to the virgin goddess, fair Juliet, since she is jealous of your beauty. Give up the vows of chastity to which Diana would bind you, and wear not her pale colors, which the wise avoid.

Oh! It is my beloved who stands there, my queen, mistress of my heart! How I long for her to know that she is so! She gives expression to her thoughts, yet she utters no sound. But that matters little, the eloquence of her eyes is all that is needed. I will reply to the thoughts I read there.

Nay, that would be presumption, her thoughts are not meant for my reading. Her shining eyes are so bright, that it would seem as though two of the loveliest stars in the firmament, having some affairs to which they wished to attend, might ask them to do duty in the sky during their absence. And, if they did ask, and took the place of my lady's eyes, even their starry brilliance would be unable to dim the beauty of that face. Its radiance would as far outshine their splendor as the sunshine overpowers a pale gleam of a candle and, in the firmament, my lady's eyes would pour forth such brightness, that the birds in those high realms would begin to trill their little songs, thinking that day had come. I see her leaning her face upon her hand. How gladly would I be the glove which she wore, so that that lovely face might rest upon me.

Juliet: Alas!

Romeo: I hear her voice! Oh! Let me hear it again, radiant spirit, for such you appear to me. Your glorious beauty, shining above me in the darkness of night, appears like some angelic being, who floats upon the slow-moving clouds, and wings his way through the air, while mortal men look upward and watch him with wondering awe.

Juliet: O, Romeo! Why is thy name Romeo? Oh, my love! Give up thy family and disown thy father. Or, if that may not be, then vow only to be my love, and I myself will forsake my father's house, and never more claim kinship with the Capulets.

Romeo: Is it wise to listen longer, or ought I to declare myself now?

Juliet: No part of him is my foe except his name. He would still be the same youth, even though he were not called Montague. His name is not really himself, it has nothing to do with any part of his person. O Romeo! Do not be a Montague! Why should a name mean so much? That lovely flower known as a "rose" would lose no part of its sweetness or scent, though it should be known by any other title. And Romeo, in the same way, would still possess all those lovable attributes that are his, were his name some other one than Montague. Put off your name, Romeo and, in exchange for that, which has, really, nothing to do with your real self, I will give you my whole self.

Romeo: I will gladly do as you say. Only let me be called your beloved, and I will take another name, and never more be known by that of Romeo.

Juliet: Who is this man, who, hidden by the dusky night, has thus chanced to overhear my secrets?

Romeo: I cannot give my name, dear saint, for the only one I can give is unpleasing to you, and therefore I myself detest it. If it were written down before me, I would destroy the writing.

Juliet: I have not yet heard a hundred words spoken by that voice, and yet I recognize its dear tones. You are Romeo, are you not? And the son of Montague?

Romeo: If it displease you, sweet lady, I will deny both those titles.

Juliet: How did you reach this place, and why did you come? The walls surrounding this garden are both lofty and difficult to scale. And, once inside them, you are face to face with death, should you be discovered by any Capulet, seeing that your house is that of our great foe.

Romeo: Love lent me wings to soar above the loftiest wall, for no mere barrier of stone can keep out love. It will always attempt the impossible. Therefore, neither high walls nor fierce kinsfolk are any hindrance to me.

Juliet: They will take your life if they discover you.

Romeo: Indeed, sweet lady, I run more risk of danger from your bright glances than from the weapons of a score of angry men. If you will only look kindly upon me, no hatred of my foes can hurt me.

Juliet: For all the wealth of the universe, I would not have them find you in this place.

Romeo: This mantle of darkness will conceal me. But, if you do not love me, I am willing to be discovered. I should prefer to meet my death here and now, by the swords of my enemies, rather than to live on, if your love be denied me.

Juliet: Who showed you the way to my home?

Romeo: Love directed me, as at his bidding I already wished to know. He gave me the wisdom, and I took the means to follow his advice. I should make but a poor sailor, yet, if you should be as far removed from me as to the desolate shores of the ocean which flows to the uttermost bounds of the earth, I would dare the voyage for such a precious freight.

Juliet: Were my features not hidden from your view by the concealing shades of night, I should blush at the remembrance of the words which you overheard tonight. Gladly would I take refuge in a formal distant behavior, and oh how gladly would I deny the words which I uttered! But that would now be useless, so away with formality and etiquette. Am I indeed your love? I know your reply will be "yes," and I believe it. Nevertheless, lovers have sworn before now, and have proved false to their vows, and Jove, it is said, counts the breaking of lovers' vows no deadly sin. Dear Romeo, if you indeed love me, tell me so in earnest truth. If you think that I have yielded too quickly, I will be wayward and capricious, and look with disapproval upon you, and deny your suit, if then you will renew your courtship, and sue for my love. But otherwise, not for the world would I behave so to my love.

Indeed, gentle Romeo, I love you too dearly, and I fear that from that you may think me fickle and capricious. But you may be assured, fair sir, that you will find me more constant than some who have more craft than I, and pretend to a distant behavior. I own that had you not overheard my words, I should myself have behaved more distantly toward you, but you had already discovered, before I knew of your presence, the depth of my love for you. Forgive me, then, and do not think me wanton because I respond so readily to your words of love, and show so plainly my affection, revealed to you by the shadows of night.

Romeo: Madam, I vow by the sacred moon, whose silvery beams lighten these orchard boughs—

Juliet: Oh! Do not liken your vows to the moon that in its revolving course presents an ever varying face, lest your affection should chance to be as changeable.

Romeo: What oath shall I take?

Juliet: Take no oath at all. Or, if it please you to swear, let it be by your own fair and gentle self, which is the object of my adoration. Then I will trust your vows.

Romeo: If my soul's deep affection—

Juliet: Nay, take no oath at all. My heart is filled with gladness, because of your love. But it also feels a dread, a foreboding of sorrow, which prevents me being completely happy in this exchange of vows. I feel that love has come upon us too suddenly, and our mutual promises are too hasty, too unconsidered. Love has flashed upon us like the lightning, which is gone again before we can well declare it has been here. Farewell, beloved, our young affection, ripened meanwhile, may grow to its full strength and beauty by the time we meet again. Good night, good night! May your heart rest in such sweet security and gladness as does mine.

Romeo: Ah! Must we part, when I long for so much more?

Juliet: What more can I bestow on you tonight?

Romeo: Promise to be true to me, as I will be to you.

Juliet: My love was given to you before you asked it. Nevertheless, I wish it were still mine to give again.

Romeo: Do you wish to take it back? Why would you do so, beloved?

Juliet: For no other reason than to have the pleasure of freely giving it once more. Yet I need not wish for it back, for I have it all the time. My love for you is as deep as the ocean, and my generosity as wide—the more I give you, the more I own myself, for it is boundless. [*Nurse calls within.*] I hear a sound from the house. Farewell, beloved one! Coming, good Nurse! Dear Montague, be faithful. Wait awhile, I will return to you.

[*Exit above.*]

Romeo: O thrice happy night! My only dread is, that this being night, I shall awaken and find this happiness has been only a vision of the night, too rapturously blissful to be a reality.

[*Re-enter Juliet, above.*]

Juliet: Only a few more words, love, and then we must in reality part for tonight. If the intention of your love toward me be honest and upright, and you mean to wed with me, I shall find tomorrow a messenger to send to you. Let me have a message, by his hand, telling me when I must meet you, and at what place you will have the ceremony performed. And I will bring you, as an offering, all my wealth, and will go henceforth with you, my king, even to the other side of the earth.

Nurse: [*Within.*] Lady!

Juliet: In a moment! But if you are only deceiving me, I beg of you—

Nurse: [*Within.*] My lady!

Juliet: In a moment! I am coming! To woo me no further, but leave me to grieve alone! I will send the messenger in the morning.

Romeo: May my soul be so dealt with—

Juliet: A thousand times good night.

[*Exit above.*]

Romeo: Night is not good, but a thousand times the worse, without your bright presence. Love flies to meet love, as schoolboys fly from their tasks. But love parts with love as reluctantly as children move toward school.

[*Retiring.*]

[*Re-enter Juliet, above.*]

Juliet: Romeo! Romeo! Listen! How I wish that my voice might entice this noble hawk back to me, as a falconer lures his bird! Those who are not free to follow their own wishes, may not call loudly for what they wish, or I would call so loudly that my voice should rend the air in Echo's cave, and force her to repeat my cries until her light, sweet voice should sound as rough as mine, with continued calling of the name of my beloved.

Romeo: My heart's beloved is repeating my name! How delightful do the tones of a loved one's voice sound, in the stillness of night! They are like silvery chimes, or faint, sweet notes of music to those that listen.

Juliet: Romeo!

Romeo: My beloved!

Juliet: At what hour shall I send my messenger?

Romeo: At nine o'clock.

Juliet: I shall be sure to send. What an age it seems until nine o'clock tomorrow! Why did I recall you? I cannot remember.

Romeo: Let me wait near you, until you recollect it.

Juliet: If you wait there, I shall never remember. I shall be able to think of nothing but that you are near me, and that I love you to be there.

Romeo: And I shall remain as long as it takes you to remember, while I shall forget that this is not my home.

Juliet: Daybreak is near. I am afraid for your life if you remain longer, and yet it would please me to be able to recall you at will, like a playful girl who ties her bird with a silken thread and, within the limits of its line, lets it have freedom, but only to bring it back at her pleasure, loving it too much to set it free forever.

Romeo: I wish that I were a bird of yours.

Juliet: Dearest, I wish the same, but I would kill you with kindness. Farewell! Farewell! It is so bittersweet to part, that I shall prolong our farewells until it be no longer good night, but good morning!

[*Exit.*]

Romeo: May sweet sleep rest on your eyelids, and peace in your bosom! I would that I could be sleep and peace, to have so dear a resting place! I will go from here to the kind priest's dwelling, and tell him of the joy which has befallen me, and beg his assistance.

[*Exit.*]

ACT II · SCENE 3

[*Friar Laurence's cell.*]

[*Enter Friar Laurence, with a basket.*]

Friar Laurence: Now cheerful daybreak puts to flight night's gloomy shades and, from the east, long shafts of dawn pierce the dark masses of cloud, until the shadows of night retreat hurriedly before the flaming wheels of the chariot of Helios, and leave a clear pathway for the god of day. Now I must hasten to fill my willow basket with herbs, both harmful and beneficial, according to their use. I must complete my task before the risen sun's burning glance dries up the dews of night, and gladdens the earth with its cheering rays. And this same earth, from which spring all the bountiful products of nature is, at the same time, the final resting place of all. Her broad bosom brings forth countless fruits of all kinds, yet it is also their sepulchre. And we mortals find, scattered over her breast and drawing their nourishment from there, many and varied herbs, of which some have many useful properties, some few. But every one has at least one virtue of its own, though each one differs from its fellow.

Oh! What wondrous and mighty good dwells in all nature—in herbs and minerals of all kinds, when turned to their right uses. There is nothing in the whole world so utterly worthless that it cannot bestow some useful gift upon the world, did we only know how to apply it. As also, there is nothing good which may not become the instrument of great harm, when turned aside from its proper use. Even the finest qualities in man may, by being wrongly employed, bring about evil results, and an evil aim may sometimes work in such a manner as to seem a benefit for the time. Enclosed within the limits of this frail and delicate blossom are powers so diverse as poison and healing—the power to refresh and the power to slay. The sweet odor of the plant cheers and refreshes the body. But, if the same herb be eaten, its deadly poison stills the heart forever. And we find the same in the human race. In every man dwell two mighty warring forces, good and evil, grace and perversity, and if the baser part of man's nature be allowed to gain the mastery, the better part dies, as a flower that decay has consumed.

[*Enter Romeo.*]

Romeo: Good morning, Father!

Friar Laurence: My blessing upon you! Whose voice is this that greets me so pleasantly at such an early hour? My boy, if you leave your couch so early in the morning, I must conclude that your mind is not at rest. Old people all have troubles and anxieties to keep them wakeful, and refreshing slumber never comes to those who are so troubled, but youthful heads unvexed by cares and worries, sleep soundly on their pillows. I know, therefore, by your presence here so early, that some disturbance of mind or body has driven you from your couch. If that is not the reason, then there is but one other explanation, which must be the true one. That is, that you have never been to rest at all.

Romeo: The latter is the correct explanation. I have had much more pleasure than if I had been asleep.

Friar Laurence: God forgive you if you have done wrong! Have you been in Rosaline's company?

Romeo: In Rosaline's company? Not I, good priest. The name of Rosaline, and all the misery I endured for her sake, has completely passed out of my remembrance.

Friar Laurence: That is well, my boy! Then where did you spend the night?

Romeo: I will answer that at once. I have been at a banquet in the house of a foe, where, suddenly, I pierced the heart of one who pierced mine in return. The cure of both our hurts lies in your hands, and you are the man who alone can aid us. It is a proof that my heart holds no malice, holy father, when I ask your aid, for my petition also includes my enemy.

Friar Laurence: Speak plainly, my son, and tell me exactly what you mean, for if I cannot understand your confession, it is impossible for me to give you a satisfactory absolution.

Romeo: Then, without more misunderstandings, I now tell you that I love Juliet, the wealthy Lord Capulet's lovely daughter, with all my heart, and she loves me as deeply in return. We are united in love for each other and nothing remains now, but the uniting of our hands in holy wedlock. Come with me, and as we go I will tell you all the course of our love, and how we at last pledged our faith to each other, but the most important point is, that I want you to agree to marry us at once.

Friar Laurence: By the blessed St. Francis! How different this tale is from the one I last heard from your lips! Have you so quickly forgotten Rosaline, whom you said you so deeply loved? Evidently a youth's affection is not very deeply seated. Ye powers above! Think of the streams of salt water that flowed down your cheeks, pale with love of Rosaline! What a waste of brine that, in the end, had no effect upon the love which caused it to flow! The vapor of your sighs has scarcely yet had time to be dispersed by the sun's rays.

The sound of your groans has not yet left my old ears, and here, I swear I find the mark of a tear yet remaining on your cheek! As surely as you were really Romeo, and all those sighs and miseries were yours, both yourself and your unhappiness belonged entirely to Rosaline. Have you so altered? Then we may well allow women to be inconstant, when even men prove themselves so fickle.

Romeo: But my love for Rosaline often incurred your displeasure.

Friar Laurence: Not your love, but your foolishness, my boy.

Romeo: You told me to put love from me.

Friar Laurence: But not to put one away and take another immediately.

Romeo: Do not be angry with me, I beg of you. The lady whom I love now meets kindness with kindness, and returns my affection, and feels as deeply as I do, which Rosaline never did.

Friar Laurence: She was wise, and knew that the affection you professed for her was merely got up, parrotlike, because you thought it was the correct thing for a young man to do. She knew that your heart did not prompt it, nor your mind understand it. It was all an affair of the lips. But I will accompany you, young changeable one, and will do the one thing you require of me. A marriage between you and your betrothed may be the means of ending the hatred which has existed so long between your two families, and may have the effect of changing bitterness into friendship.

Romeo: Hasten! Let us go at once. Our success depends on our speed.

Friar Laurence: Hasten slowly, my son. The more haste, the less speed.

[*Exit.*]

ACT II · SCENE 4

[*A street.*]

[*Enter Benvolio and Mercutio.*]

Mercutio: What in the world has become of Romeo? Did he go home last night?

Benvolio: His servant told me that he had not been at his father's house.

Mercutio: He will certainly lose his wits for love of that white-faced lady Rosaline, who is so unkind to him.

Benvolio: Old Lord Capulet's nephew, Tybalt, has written to Romeo. The letter has come to Montague's house.

Mercutio: He has challenged Romeo, I'll swear!

Benvolio: Romeo will not be afraid to reply.

Mercutio: Anyone who knows how to write can reply to a letter.

Benvolio: I do not mean the letter, it is the writer of it that Romeo will answer. He will dare to reply to the man who has dared him to fight.

Mercutio: But poor Romeo has already been slain, conquered by the dark eyes of a pale-faced maid, overcome by an amorous song and pierced to the heart by an arrow from Cupid's bow. How can such a one meet Tybalt in a duel?

Benvolio: What is there so remarkable about Tybalt? Who is he?

Mercutio: Something more than a storybook hero, you can depend. On my word, he is the valiant leader of your men of niceties! He fights by rule, and attends strictly to detail. He is a master of precision—every beat has its appropriate movement, and before you know it, his sword's point is at your heart. He will pierce you a silk button most accurately—a master of the duel, a man foremost among those who stand on formalities in the conduct of quarrels. Ah! Their wonderful advances, retreats and thrusts!

Benvolio: Their what?

Mercutio: A plague on these fellows, with their affected jargon, these inventors of new terms! Do you not think it most annoying, old friend, that we should be tormented by these buzzing insects, these inventors of new fashions, with their artificial mannerisms and pretences of courtesy, who are so particular about the latest fashion that ordinary behavior will not suffice them. Oh! Their French phrases!

[*Enter Romeo.*]

Benvolio: Here he is, here comes Romeo himself.

Mercutio: Only half of himself, like a smoked herring deprived of its eggs. Nothing less than verse will satisfy him now. He will write sonnets to his lady, as Petrarch did to his Laura, who, in Romeo's eyes, was no better than a servant when compared with Rosaline. But, in faith, Laura had a more learned lover to write poetry for her! And, further, to compare with Rosaline, the lovely queen of Carthage was plain and homely, Cleopatra of Egypt a dusky-hued creature, Helen of Troy and lovely Hero, for whom Leander lost his life, were but wanton fillies, and Thisbe, a lady whose gray eyes may have bewitched Pyramus, but were nothing when matched with Rosaline's—Signior Romeo, *bon jour*! There is a French greeting for you, to suit your French garments. You deceived us finely last night!

Romeo: Good morning, friends! When did I deceive you?

Mercutio: When you gave us the slip, my friend. Do you not understand?

Romeo: Forgive me, good Mercutio, but I had a most important affair to attend to and, under the circumstances, one may be excused if he does not stand on ceremony occasionally.

Mercutio: Then circumstances such as yours make people bend the knee.

Romeo: That is, makes them curtsy.

Mercutio: You put it most accurately.

Romeo: A very courteous explanation.

Mercutio: Oh! I am the pink of politeness.

Romeo: That is the flower of it.

Mercutio: Exactly!

Romeo: Then my shoe is well "pinked."

Mercutio: Very good! Follow up the pun until your shoe is worn out, then the joke is the "sole" thing that will remain.

Romeo: What a threadbare pun! Its only merit is its singularity.

Mercutio: Kind Benvolio, part us now! My brain gives way!

Romeo: Nay, keep it up! Keep it up! Our wits are fairly measured.

Mercutio: Oh, if we are to play a wild-goose chase with our wits, you will win easily, for all my wits put together are not so wild as one of yours! Did I touch you there with goose?

Romeo: You never fail to touch me with goose for, whenever you are with me, you are one!

Mercutio: I will pay you out for saying that!

Romeo: Nay, do not so, dear goose.

Mercutio: Yours is a biting wit, as keen as it is amusing—a good sauce.

Romeo: Then you ought to appreciate it when served up to well-flavored goose!

Mercutio: Here is a pliant wit, that can stretch out to any length!

Romeo: So it stretches out to accommodate your large phrases, and prove you a large kind of goose.

Mercutio: Now, do you not find this a pleasanter pastime than groaning for love? You are more agreeable, more like yourself! Now you show yourself as you really are. But when you are moping and moaning for love, you merely resemble a fool, a jester wandering about looking for a hiding place for his fool's head!

Benvolio: There! There! Let that end your discussion!

Mercutio: You rub me up in my "tale" against the grain.

Benvolio: Otherwise your "tail" would have been too long!

Mercutio: Nay, you are quite mistaken. It would have been brief, for I had exhausted the subject and meant to say no more about it.

Romeo: Here's a fine sight!

[*Enter Nurse and Peter.*]

Mercutio: A ship! A ship!

Benvolio: A couple of them—male and female!

Nurse: Peter!

Peter: Here!

Nurse: Give me my fan, Peter.

Mercutio: Yes, do, good fellow! Let it cover her face, for it is the better looking of the two.

Nurse: Good morning, sirs.

Mercutio: Give you good even, beauteous lady!

Nurse: Is it good even?

Mercutio: It really is, I assure you. Time's thieving hand is even now overtaking the hour of noon.

Nurse: Bah, sir, what a man you are!

Romeo: He is a man, madam, whom the Creator made very well, but he, himself, spoils his Maker's handiwork.

Nurse: You say truly, indeed, that he spoils his Maker's handiwork as you say. Can any of you, sirs, tell me where I may find young Signior Romeo?

Romeo: Yes, I can inform you of that. However, he will not be such a young Romeo when you find him, as he was when you set out to look for him. I myself am called Romeo, and I am the youngest Romeo there is, for want of a worse.

Nurse: You say well.

Mercutio: Indeed! Is the worst well? Very well answered, on my word! Very good indeed!

Nurse: If you are Romeo, young signior, I wish to have some talk with you.

Benvolio: She is going to invite him to supper.

Mercutio: O ho! so, she is a temptress, is she?

Romeo: What have you found?

Mercutio: I have not found a hare, sir, unless it be something old and past its prime, like a hare in a Lenten pie.

An old gray hare, and an old gray hare,
May be suitable fare in Lent;
But for a hare that is gray we'd rather not stay,
Our time might be far better spent.

Are you coming home, Romeo? We are going to dine at your father's house.

Romeo: I will come afterwards.

Mercutio: Adieu, aged madam! Adieu! [*Singing.*] *"Lady, lady lady!"*

[*Exit Mercutio and Benvolio.*]

Nurse: Adieu, indeed! Who is this forward young fellow, I ask you, who was so full of roguery?

Romeo: A young signior, nurse, who is exceedingly fond of the sound of his own voice, and who lets his tongue run away with his wits.

Nurse: If his tongue has anything to say against me, I will make him feel small, were he ever such a big, strong fellow. I will take the conceit out of him, and a score like him, and if I should be unable to do it, there are many who would do it for me. Low fellow! I am no base companion of his, that he should speak so to me. [*To Peter.*] And all you could do was to stand quietly there, and allow any villain to do as he liked with me!

Peter: I never saw any man doing as he liked with you. Had that been the case, I should have very soon drawn my sword, I can tell you. You will not find me more backward than anyone else, if I have a good reason for fighting, and can do so without breaking the law.

Nurse: On my faith. I feel so angry that I am trembling from head to foot! Worthless villain! I ask you, young sir, listen to me. I was telling you that my young mistress sent me to look for you, but I will not tell you the message she gave me. I will first of all say to you that if you should deceive her, and lead her to think that her happiness was safe in your hands, and then disappoint her, as the saying is, it would be very mean conduct on your part, as the saying is, for the lady is but a girl yet, and so it would be most evil behavior if you should trick her, and a very dreadful wrong to be offered to any lady.

Romeo: Give my compliments, nurse, to the young lady whom you serve. I declare to you—

Nurse: Kind soul! And, on my word, I will let my lady know what you say. Heavens! How delighted she will be!

Romeo: What will you let her know? I am afraid you are paying little attention to my words.

Nurse: I will say that you declare, and that is a most handsome offer, as I understand it.

Romeo: Ask her to contrive to be allowed to come this afternoon to Friar Laurence's cell, to confession. When she is there, she shall have absolution, and also will be wedded to me. Take this, for your trouble.

Nurse: Indeed, no, signior. I will take nothing.

Romeo: Nonsense! You must take it.

Nurse: I will see that she comes at the time you say.

Romeo: And listen, my dear nurse. In less than an hour my servant will come to you, bringing you a rope ladder. This ladder I will use when hidden by the darkness of night. It shall be my pathway to the summit of my bliss and delight. Adieu! Do not fail me, and your trouble shall be rewarded. Farewell! Give my compliments to your lady.

Nurse: Heaven be gracious to you, young sir. But listen!

Romeo: Kind nurse, what do you wish to say?

Nurse: Will your servant not betray you? Have you never heard the saying that it is easy for two to keep a secret if only one knows it?

Romeo: No one could be more faithful than my servant is.

Nurse: That is well. My young lady is the most beautiful thing— Heaven! I can remember when she was but a tiny, lisping child. Oh, I must tell you that a young nobleman of this city, Paris, would dearly like to capture this prize. But the dear girl herself would as willingly look upon an ugly toad, as upon him. I now and then vex her by saying that Paris is a more handsome man than yourself, but when I say that, I declare to you that she turns as white as a cloth. Does not the same letter begin both your name and the word "rosemary"?

Romeo: Yes, the letter "R" begins both words. What then?

Nurse: Now you are joking with me? "R" is the dog's letter. Nay, I am sure that was not the letter. At any rate, my little lady has so pleasing a saying about you and rosemary, that you would be delighted to hear it.

Romeo: Remember me to your mistress.

Nurse: Indeed I will, most willingly. [*Exit Romeo.*] Peter!

Peter: Coming!

Nurse: You run on in front, and make haste!

[*Exit.*]

ACT II · SCENE 5

[*Capulet's orchard.*]

[*Enter Juliet.*]

Juliet: Nurse gave me her word she would be back in half an hour, and it was exactly upon the stroke of nine when I sent her forth. It may be that she has not found him, but no! I will not believe that. Oh, how slow she is. The messengers of Cupid ought to be thoughts, which fly more swiftly than sunshine chases shadow from the slopes of cloudswept heights. That is why Venus' chariot is drawn by swift-winged doves, and that is why fleet young Cupid, who travels swiftly as the wind, has wings. The sun has now reached the highest point of his daily travels, and it is noon. And yet Nurse has not returned, although three tedious hours have passed since she went out. If she had the warmth and ardor of youthful passions, she would move as quickly as a ball, and the eagerness of our messages should strike her swiftly back and forth between my beloved and me. But the movements of aged people are as slow and labored, as though they had no life in their limbs, but were already dead.

[*Enter Nurse and Peter.*]

O heavens! Here she is! Oh, dear, sweet Nurse, what tidings have you for me? Did you see him? Tell your servant to go.

Nurse: Peter, go outside and wait.

[*Exit Peter.*]

Juliet: Now, dear, kind Nurse! Oh, me! Why have you such a sorrowful expression? If your news be sorrowful, still be cheerful in telling it, and if it be glad tidings, then you spoil the sweet sound by using a gloomy face as the instrument by which to convey it.

Nurse: Excuse me for a few moments, I am utterly worn out! My legs fairly ache! I have had a journey.

Juliet: I would willingly exchange my limbs for your news. Tell me, I beg of you, what you have to say, dear Nurse, tell me quickly!

Nurse: Dear me! What a hurry for news! Can you not wait a moment? Do you not see that I have scarcely breath enough to speak to you?

Juliet: How can that be, when you are speaking to me all the time? You are wasting more time and breath in putting off your message, than it would have taken to tell me the whole story. At any rate, say first of all whether you bring good or bad tidings. Only tell me which, and I will wait patiently for details, but do not keep me in suspense any longer as to which it is.

Nurse: Here's a fine, foolish choice that you have made! You know nothing of how to select a husband. As for Romeo—oh, dear, no, nothing of the kind! His face may be as handsome as anyone else's, but his limbs are more handsome still and, as for his hands, feet and himself generally, they may be nothing much to speak of, and yet they are finer than any I have seen. He may not be the very essence of fine manners, but I dare swear he is gentle and kind. Run away now, child, and be a good girl. Is dinner over?

Juliet: No, not yet. But I know quite well all that you are telling me. I want to hear what Romeo said about our being married. What did he say to you?

Nurse: Oh, heavens! What a headache I have! My head is throbbing as though it would burst. And now my back aches! A plague on you for sending me on such an errand! This running to and fro has pretty well killed me.

Juliet: Truly, Nurse, I am grieved that it should have tired you so much. But dear, kind and good Nurse, do tell me what my beloved says.

Nurse: He speaks like a worthy gentleman, and a civil, gracious and noble-looking one, and good—I dare swear it—is your mother in?

Juliet: Of course she is. Where do you think she would be? What a curious way to answer my question! You say my love speaks like a worthy gentleman, and then ask whether my mother is in!

Nurse: By the blessed Virgin, how hasty you are! Indeed, young lady! Is this all the reward I get for my pains? After this, I'll leave you to do your own errands.

Juliet: What a tremendous fuss! Come, tell me at once, what did Romeo say?

Nurse: Are you to be allowed to go to confession today?

Juliet: Yes.

Nurse: Then hurry away to the dwelling of Friar Laurence, and there you will find a husband awaiting you, ready to make you his wife. Ah! That makes your cheeks flame, they blush readily at my news of Romeo. Now hasten to the ceremony. I must go in another direction to get a ladder, which your lover will use, when night falls, to climb up to the nest of his little bird. I have all the heavy work to do in order to serve your pleasure, but your turn will come. Go now. Hasten to Friar Laurence, and I will go and dine.

Juliet: I hasten to my happiness. Adieu, trusty Nurse!

[*Exit.*]

ACT II · SCENE 6

[*Friar Laurence's cell.*]

[*Enter Friar Laurence and Romeo.*]

Friar Laurence: Heaven grant that this sacred ceremony we are about to engage in may be so pleasing to the powers above, that we shall not, in the future, have to regret that it was accomplished.

Romeo: God grant it! Amen! But no matter what misfortunes may overtake me, or what anguish I may have to bear, the bliss of even one moment of her companionship would outweigh it all. When once our hands have been united by the sacred words which you will pronounce, then death, the destroyer of love, may do its worst. The joy of possessing her makes amends for all.

Friar Laurence: But, too frequently, the love which is one great blaze of passion ends as abruptly as it began. The fulfilment of the longed-for desire brings about its own end, even as the coming together of fire and powder results in their mutual destruction. The taste is deadened by the excessive sweetness of honey, and the enjoyment of it fails from that very excess of sweetness. Therefore, avoid extremes, and in your love be temperate—the most enduring affection is moderate in its expression, and a passion that outruns all wisdom ends by burning itself out, and having as little to show in the end, as one that has been distant and cool from the beginning.

[*Enter Juliet.*]

Your lady approaches. That dainty footstep will never make an impression on the stony pavement. But lovers are so buoyed up by the thoughts of their loved ones that they seem to walk on air, and even the cobweb threads that idly wave in the summer breeze, seem strong enough to bear them.

Juliet: Good evening, my spiritual father.

Friar Laurence: I will leave Romeo to thank you for both of us.

Juliet: Greeting to him also, then, or he would be thanking me for something he had not received!

Romeo: Beloved lady, speak, if your cup of bliss seems, as mine does, to be filled to overflowing, and if you can find better words than I in which to paint our happiness. Let the perfume of your breath and the glorious tones of your sweet voice fill the surrounding air, while you declare the rapture that fills our hearts, at this precious opportunity of meeting.

Juliet: The thoughts which are filled with joyful realities, as mine are, are not dependent on mere phrases to show their worth. They are prouder of the matter which they enshrine, than of any flowery orations in which it may be set forth. The love that can be all set down in language and summed up, cannot be very great. My own is so boundless that I cannot express even half of it.

Friar Laurence: Let us go at once, and perform the ceremony quickly. I shall not leave you now until the sacred words have been spoken in the holy temple, which shall unite you to each other, and make you one.

[*Exit.*]

ACT III · SCENE 1

[*Verona, a public place.*]
[*Enter Mercutio, Benvolio, a page and servants.*]

Benvolio: Dear Mercutio, do let me persuade you to leave the streets. There are many of Capulet's household roaming about, and if we chance to encounter them we are sure to be drawn into a quarrel. In this hot weather men's passions are very easily roused.

Mercutio: You remind me of a man who walks into an inn and lays his drawn sword on the table, saying he hopes to heaven he will not need to use it, but who, by the time he has finished his second glass, is ready to turn it against the waiter without the slightest provocation.

Benvolio: Do you think me such a one as that?

Mercutio: Well, you know that you are as fiery a fellow as any in the land, and are as easily provoked to ill humor as any, and as readily in the mood to be provoked.

Benvolio: Provoked to what?

Mercutio: Two? There would never be two of such people, for each would soon slay the other, then there would be none. You are so ready to quarrel that so slight a cause as the number of hairs in a man's beard will serve as a pretext, or the fact that you see him eating nuts, when your eyes are hazel. No one but you would ever think of such a reason for quarrelling! You seem to think of nothing else but squabbling, although I should have thought you had been punished sufficiently to know better. A man who coughed in the street and roused your dog from his nap in the warm sunshine has angered you before now. You have wrangled with a tailor for putting on his new clothes before Easter, and with another man for only fastening his new shoes with old ribbon. And yet, you take it upon yourself to advise me to avoid quarrels!

Benvolio: If I were as ready to be drawn into brawls as you are, anyone who liked might purchase the absolute right to my life, and I would sell it to him, for I should have but a short time to live.

Mercutio: Foolish fellow!

Benvolio: By my head, here are some of our foes approaching.

Mercutio: By my foot, I do not care if they are!

[Enter Tybalt and others.]

Tybalt: I shall accost these Montagues, so keep near to me. Good evening, sirs, I should like a word with one of you!

Mercutio: Only one word? And with only one of us? Make it more than that. Let us say two—a word and a blow!

Tybalt: If you give me a reason to give the blow, you will not find me at all unwilling to do it.

Mercutio: Oh, do not wait for me to give you reason! Can you not take it yourself?

Tybalt: Then here it is: you, Mercutio, are frequently found consorting with Romeo.

Mercutio: Consorting? Do you think we are wandering musicians? If we are, then I am afraid you will hear a few discords. And this will be the instrument I will make you dance to! Consort, indeed!

Benvolio: Do not quarrel here, where everyone can see us! Either talk more quietly or choose some less crowded thoroughfare for your squabbles. Or else leave each other, and go away. You are attracting everyone's attention.

Mercutio: They are free to give us their attention, if they wish. Their eyes are for the purpose of looking, I suppose. In any case, I shall not move from here to please other people!

[Enter Romeo.]

Tybalt: I will leave you at peace, sir, this is my man approaching.

Mercutio: He wears no livery of yours, I vow! The only way in which your highness might claim him as your man would be that Romeo would quickly follow you to a field, if you challenge him to fight.

Tybalt: My feelings toward you, Romeo, are such that the only name I can find for you is—knave!

Romeo: My feelings toward you, Tybalt, are at the present moment most friendly. The cause of their being so kindly disposed toward you is so precious to me, that it induces me to refrain from the anger, which I should otherwise feel at your manner of addressing me. I am no knave, however. I will therefore leave you. I see your idea of my character is entirely a mistaken one.

Tybalt: Those excuses, young man, will not satisfy my anger or remove the cause of it. Stay where you are, and draw your sword!

Romeo: I declare that I have never done you harm, and so far from wishing to do so, I have a warmer regard for you than you can ever imagine, until you learn the cause of my kindly feelings. Therefore, be content, my dear Capulet, for I can assure you I respect your name as much as I do my own.

Mercutio: You want to get out of it, do you, you wretched coward? Afraid of a rapier thrust, are you? [*Draws his sword.*] All right! Here, Tybalt, you low-down dog, I'll try you.

Tybalt: What do you want with me?

Mercutio: All I want, you miserable animal, is to give you a lesson to go on with. What I shall do, afterwards, will depend on the way you behave yourself. Well, are you going to draw your weapon or not? You had better hurry up, else you'll feel the weight of mine before you are ready for it.

Tybalt: All right, I am ready!

[*Drawing his sword.*]

Romeo: My dear Mercutio, sheathe your weapon. Do not fight him.

Mercutio: Come, sir! Begin!

[*They fight.*]

Romeo: Benvolio, out with your sword, and strike theirs down! You ought to be ashamed, sirs, to fight thus! Cease this mad brawling! Tybalt! Mercutio! You know that the prince has distinctly forbidden fighting in the streets. Tybalt, stop! Stop, Mercutio!

[*Exit Tybalt and his partisans.*]

Mercutio: I am wounded! Confound your quarrels! I am done for! Has he escaped, and without a scratch?

Benvolio: Why, Mercutio! Has he wounded you?

Mercutio: Yes! I am afraid he has scratched me this time! Is my servant there? Run, you young rascal, and bring a doctor.

[*Exit page.*]

Romeo: Oh come, you cannot be seriously wounded, Mercutio. Keep up your spirits!

Mercutio: Well, the wound certainly does not look very serious, but I am afraid I shall find it so, in spite of its appearance. I reckon I'm done for this time. Pest take you and your feuds! Oh, to think that I have met my death by the hand of such a creature, who is not even a skilful swordsman, but who fights by rule! Why, in the fiend's name, did you interfere? He took the opportunity to stab me under cover of your arm.

Romeo: I did what I thought was the best thing to do.

Mercutio: Lend me your aid, Benvolio. Take me indoors somewhere or I shall faint. Curse your quarrels! They have forced me to feed the worms! I have got it, most thoroughly—your quarrels!

[*Exit Mercutio and Benvolio.*]

Romeo: Mercutio, my dear friend, a near relative of the prince, is wounded to death for my sake, and my good name is slandered by Tybalt's lies—Tybalt, who, for an hour, has been my relative. O beautiful Juliet, your lovely image fills my heart, leaving no room in it for strife, so that I fear I must seem to have lost all manly spirit and courage, and appear to bend like a faulty sword.

[*Re-enter Benvolio.*]

Benvolio: Alas, Romeo, gallant Mercutio is slain! The spirit of that fearless, noble youth, too soon forsaking this world, has soared to the skies!

Romeo: The shadow of this evil day will hang over many a day to come. This sad event is but the beginning of the misery which I foresee in the future!

[*Re-enter Tybalt.*]

Benvolio: Here is that fierce Capulet returning!

Romeo: What! Still living? And rejoicing in his evil work? And my dear friend lies dead by his hand! Begone from my heart, all feelings of consideration. Here, Tybalt, do I throw back in your teeth the name of villain, which you applied to me just now. The spirit of Mercutio waits above us, hovering near until your soul also is sent from this world. One of us, perhaps both, will join him soon.

Tybalt: Miserable youth, it is your soul that I will send to bear him company there, as you did on earth!

Romeo: Well, we will let this settle it.

[*They fight; Tybalt falls.*]

Benvolio: Fly, Romeo, fly! Tybalt is dead. The whole city is roused, and you will be sentenced to death by the prince, if you do not escape. Oh, hasten, do not linger a moment!

Romeo: Oh! I am the plaything of fate! The sport of circumstance!

Benvolio: Why do you not go?

[Exit Romeo.]

[Enter citizens, etc.]

First Citizen: Where is that murderer, Tybalt, who has slain Mercutio? In what direction did he go?

Benvolio: He lies before you!

First Citizen: Come, sir, along with me. In the prince's name, do not resist.

[Enter prince with attendants, Montague, Capulet, their wives and others.]

Prince: Where are the villains who began this brawling?

Benvolio: Most worthy prince, I can tell you all about this fatal quarrel, and how it came about. The murderer of Mercutio, your relative, is lying there, struck down in his turn by the hand of Romeo.

Lady Capulet: O Tybalt, my kinsman! Prince! Husband! My brother's son is slain! O Tybalt! Tybalt! For the sake of justice, prince, and as you are an honorable man, make the life of a Montague pay for the life of this Capulet, here slain!

Prince: Who struck the first blow in this fatal quarrel, Benvolio?

Benvolio: Tybalt, who now lies before you dead. Romeo slew him. But first he had used every means to divert Tybalt from the quarrel. With fair and courteous words he begged him to consider what a petty thing it was to wrangle thus, and reminded him of the offence it was against your highness' decree. But all this gentle pleading had no effect on Tybalt's ungovernable rage, nor could Romeo persuade him to listen to words of reconciliation. He turned his keen weapon against Mercutio's heart, and Mercutio, equally fiery, met steel with steel. They thrust and parried, gave and returned swift blows, with skill and warlike courage.

Romeo tried to separate them, and, rushing between, crying out to them to cease, he swiftly struck down their deadly weapons even while he spoke. At that instant, Tybalt dealt a wicked stroke beneath Romeo's arm at gallant Mercutio, inflicting a mortal wound, and, forthwith, fled from the place. He soon returned, however, and Romeo, who, in the meantime, had been roused to fierce anger by the death of his friend, desired eagerly to avenge him, rushed upon him with drawn sword and, in an instant, they were fighting desperately. Before I even had time to unsheath my sword to separate them, Tybalt had received his fatal wound and Romeo instantly turned and escaped. On my life, this is a true account of the matter.

Lady Capulet: This man belongs to the same family as Romeo, and his love for his friend has colored his tale, making him convey a false impression. There were a score or more who took part in this wicked quarrel, and yet all their combined efforts only succeeded in killing one Capulet. Prince, I beg you for a just sentence on the murderer Romeo. Let his life pay for the life he has taken.

Prince: Tybalt took Mercutio's life, and you wish Romeo also to be slain for him. Who else must lose his life for the sake of this precious youth?

Montague: Sire, spare Romeo's life, for he, although he avenged his friend, only did what the law would otherwise have done, when he took Tybalt's life.

Prince: And, because he did so, my decree is that he be instantly banished from the city. The consequences of your quarrels have affected me also, for here lies one of my kinsmen dead through your wranglings. I will fine you both so heavily that you will mourn, at least, that a kinsman of mine should have lost his life in this fight. It will be useless to beg for a more lenient judgment. I shall ignore all you may say, nor shall any entreaties move me to overlook your offences again, therefore spare yourselves the pains. See to it that Romeo leaves Verona immediately, for if he shows himself again in the city, he shall die. Remove the body of Tybalt, and come to me to receive your sentence—when leniency is shown to murderers, it makes the judge a partner in the crime.

[*Exit.*]

ACT III · SCENE 2

[*Capulet's orchard.*]

[*Enter Juliet.*]

Juliet: Speed swiftly on, heavenly steed, shod with flame, speed on toward the west, where the sun sinks nightly into the ocean. Were the son of Helios once more your driver, he would use his lash and urge you forward with rapid pace toward your journey's end, so that dusky night might reign over the world. Enfold the earth, o night, in your shadowy mantle, so that no wandering eyes may spy my Romeo's approach, but that he may spring to my embrace, unmarked by any glances except my own, and unmolested by malicious tongues. Lovers need no light but their own loveliness, or if it be true that love is blind, then the darkness of night can make no difference in such a case. Quiet and dark-robed night, draw near, and teach me to lose myself to win my lover. Hide the fleeting red and white of my cheeks, evidence of my fluttering pulses, beneath your dusky cloak, until I cease to fear the unfamiliar nearness of my love, remembering that I am in my husband's arms.

Come, longed-for night. Romeo, draw near, thou brightness in the midst of darkness. Thy beauty will shine through the shadows of night, as a snowflake upon the raven's ebony plumes. Sweet night, draw near. Come, dear and dusky night, and bring my love to me, and when his life on earth is over, take him to your black skies, and set him there as stars amid the darkness. Then would the nightly aspect of the heavens be so beautiful, that the inhabitants of earth would wish it night forever, that they might always see such beauty, and the dazzling, showy sun would be left without honor from men. Now I own a beauteous house of love, and also my love owns me. The hours that must pass before we can meet again seem as tiresome as the hours before a festival day to some child who longs for the day to come, so that she may be arrayed in the fine new garments which she longs to wear. Oh! Nurse has returned, and with tidings of my love. The mere sound of his name on the tongue is celestial music.

[*Enter Nurse, with cords.*]

What tidings have you, Nurse? Are these the cords that Romeo spoke of?

Nurse: Yes, I have brought the cords.

[*Throws them down.*]

Juliet: Oh! What bad news have you to tell? Why do you show such signs of sorrow?

Nurse: Alas! Alas! He is slain! He's slain! We are ruined, madam. Alas! He's slain, he's gone!

Juliet: Surely fate has not dealt so cruel a blow!

Nurse: Fate did not, but Romeo did. Who could have imagined such a thing? Oh, Romeo!

Juliet: Are you a fiend, to keep me in such torturing suspense? It might well be one of the torments of Hades! Tell me, has Romeo killed himself? Only say one word, and if that word be "ay," then that short sound will deal more certain death than the poisonous glance of a serpent. No longer will I be myself if "ay" be your answer, of if his dear eyes be closed in death, so that you must say to me, "ay." Tell me at once. Is Romeo slain? Say "ay" or "no," and, by that little word, pronounce my fate!

Nurse: My own eyes were witnesses. I looked upon the wound on his bosom. Alas! I saw the woeful sight: his poor, dead body, all smeared with blood, and his pale face. My senses left me when I looked upon it.

Juliet: O break, my heart! Poor heart, that has nothing left in the whole world, but has lost all! Eyes, remain closed forever to all other sights, since you can never more look on the one you love! Worthless, wretched body, return to the earth to which you are similar. Let all movement and life end here and now, and my Romeo and I both die together!

Nurse: Alas! That Tybalt should be slain, my best friend! O worthy Tybalt, that ever I should have to mourn his death!

Juliet: What tempest of woe is overwhelming us! Tybalt, my dear cousin, killed, and Romeo, my beloved husband, slain? The last trumpet must be about to summon the world to judgment! If Romeo and my cousin be dead, who are left alive for me?

Nurse: Tybalt is dead, and Romeo, who slew him, is under sentence of banishment.

Juliet: O heaven! Was it Romeo who killed Tybalt?

Nurse: Alas! Alas! It was.

Juliet: O viper's heart, behind so fair a face! Was there ever so beautiful a dwelling that sheltered such a beast of prey? O beauteous monster! Heavenly demon! Carrion crow, wearing the plumage of the bird of peace! Greedy gentleness! Worthless, base nature in an angelic form! The very contradiction of all that appearances seem most truly to promise. A wicked saint! An upright, honest knave! O nature! What took you to the world of evil to seek out such a devilish spirit, and cause it to inhabit so fair an earthly form? Did ever a volume with so beautiful an exterior, enclose contents so evil? Oh! To think that so splendid a dwelling should harbor such guile!

Nurse: It is useless to look for either faith, loyalty or truth in men. They are all alike, lying, false and untrustworthy. Bring me a drop of brandy, sir! These sad afflictions and tribulations make me feel my weakness! Shame upon Romeo!

Juliet: How dare you speak so of him! Romeo is incapable of doing a shameful deed. He is the most honorable, and the most worthy of honor in the whole world! And yet I have been speaking ill of him, miserable creature that I am!

Nurse: Have you still any good to say of the man who slew your kinsman?

Juliet: What evil should I say of the man who is my husband? My poor husband, who will speak well of you, when even I, your new bride, have been slandering you? But why, oh knave, did you slay my kinsman? Because that knavish kinsman would have taken your life! I will weep no more, then, for tears are signs of grief, and, now, are flowing mistakenly when my heart is glad. Romeo lives, though Tybalt sought his life, and Tybalt is slain, who would have killed him. This should give me joy. Yet, still my tears are flowing, and I must wonder why. Some word was said which pierced me to the heart, and dealt a deeper wound than my kinsman's death. I long to forget it, but it lies heavy on my heart, and returns to my mind insistently, as to a criminal returns the memory of his crime.

"Tybalt is slain," they tell me, "and Romeo exiled." That is my grief—that word "exiled" has swallowed up any sorrow I could feel at the death of hundreds of kinsmen such as Tybalt. His death was a sufficient grief, had that been all. Or, if harsh grief demand others to go with it, and must have other sorrows to bear it company, then why did I not hear the tidings following my cousin's death, that either of my parents, or both, were dead also? That might have caused an ordinary sorrow. But to hear first of Tybalt's death and, then immediately afterwards, of Romeo's banishment, is woe to the uttermost—woe, which includes all that death could bring! Romeo is banished! O grief unspeakable, boundless and infinite! Where are my parents, Nurse?

Nurse: Lamenting over the dead body of your cousin. I will take you to them, if you wish.

Juliet: Are they shedding tears for Tybalt? I shall shed mine for grief at Romeo's banishment, long after theirs have ceased. Pick up the ropes. They share in my disappointment and grief. Poor steps of cord! They were fashioned to provide a path for Romeo. He is banished, and I shall die, missing his presence. I will go to my bridal chamber, but death, instead of Romeo, is my bridegroom!

Nurse: Yes, hasten to your chamber, but I will seek Romeo to console you. I know where to find him. He has taken refuge with Friar Laurence, in that good man's cell. I will go there, and, believe me, you shall see your love tonight.

Juliet: Oh! Do so, and give my faithful love this ring of mine, and tell him to come to see me, before we must part forever.

[*Exit.*]

ACT III · SCENE 3

[*Friar Laurence's cell.*]

[*Enter Friar Laurence.*]

Friar Laurence: Stand forth, Romeo. Thou terrible youth, come near. Sorrow is in love with you, and misery is your mate!

[*Enter Romeo.*]

Romeo: What tidings, father? What sentence has the prince pronounced upon me? Is there, yet, some fresh woe that I must know, which I am yet ignorant of?

Friar Laurence: My beloved son has had already too much acquaintance with such harsh and bitter fellowship. I have come to tell you the sentence of the prince.

Romeo: What else could his judgment be, but death?

Friar Laurence: A more merciful sentence issued from his lips. His sentence is not death, but exile.

Romeo: Exile! Nay, be kind, and tell me it is death. Death has a far less terrible aspect than exile. It cannot be exile!

Friar Laurence: You are banished from Verona! But have courage! All the whole wide universe is before you.

Romeo: There is nothing to me beyond the walls of this city—nothing but misery and wretchedness. To be exiled from

Verona is to be exiled from all the world I care about, and to be exiled from the world is death. Then exile is only another name for death. In calling death merely exile, you give me the reality of death with a pretence of something better. I am still slain, but you ask me to give thanks for it!

Friar Laurence: O wicked ingratitude! The lawful penalty for your offence is death. But the prince, in his mercy, has, in his generosity to you, overruled the law, and substituted banishment for the terrible sentence of death, and yet you will not appreciate the favor.

Romeo: It is no favor, but a misery. Here in Verona, is my Paradise, for Juliet dwells within its walls. Oh, to think that every mean and lowly creature within the city may see her, while I shall be forbidden such joy! It is a greater privilege, a higher honor, to be even a common fly than to be Romeo, for even an insect like that may touch the snowy hands of Juliet, or taste the divine sweetness of her lips, which, though they are so pure and chaste, glow with crimson, as though they blushed at meeting each other in a kiss. But such bliss Romeo cannot share, for he is to be exiled! When such lowly and insignificant creatures may taste such rapture, while I am removed from any share in it, can you still repeat that banishment is any better than death? Had you nothing quicker to slay me with? No deadly drink, or fatal steel, to end my life? Nothing but that dread word "exile"? O father, the lost souls know that word, and wail when it is used! How could you, my father, my sworn friend, a holy priest, a spiritual adviser and the giver of absolution, have the heart to bruise me with that terrible word, "exile"?

Friar Laurence: Foolish, crazy youth, listen to me!

Romeo: No, for you will tell me again that I am exiled.

Friar Laurence: I will give you what will prove a defence to you against it. I will teach you a philosophy, the wholesome and agreeable fruit of misfortune, that will bring you consolation, even in exile.

Romeo: "Exile" again! Away with your reasoning! Of what comfort is such reasoning to me, unless it can create a Juliet, sweep away the city of Verona or repeal a sentence, once pronounced? If it can do none of these things, it is of no use. Therefore, say no more.

Friar Laurence: I perceive that you will not listen to reason. Crazy youths will not hear!

Romeo: How can you expect it, when calm, sober people will not see?

Friar Laurence: Come, let us discuss this affair quietly.

Romeo: How can you discuss what you could never understand? Were you in my place and, had you my youth, and loved Capulet's fair daughter, and she had been but this day married to you, yet, since then, you had killed a kinsman of hers and been yourself sentenced to banishment; then, loving her to distraction as I do, you might talk of your feelings. Then, you would understand, you would show every sign of grief and measure your length upon the earth as I do, as though ready now for the tomb.

[*Knocking within.*]

Friar Laurence: Dear Romeo, get up and conceal yourself, someone wishes to enter!

Romeo: I will not hide, unless the vapors of my heavy sighs will hide me!

[*Knocking.*]

Friar Laurence: Listen! They knock again. Who is that? Romeo! Do not lie there, they will find you and arrest you! In a moment! Romeo, get up!

[*Knocking.*]

Hasten to my study. Presently! In Heaven's name, why are you so obstinate? Coming! Coming!

[*Knocking.*]

Who is that, knocking so impatiently? Where do you come from, and what do you want?

Nurse: [*Within.*] If you will admit me, I will tell you. The lady Juliet sent me.

Friar Laurence: In that case, I am glad to see you.

[*Enter Nurse.*]

Nurse: Good priest, pray tell me where Romeo is. Where is my lady's husband?

Friar Laurence: There he lies, stretched upon the earth, exhausted by his griefs.

Nurse: Alas! He is as wretched as my lady. O piteous similarity in grief. O miserable state! Just so, did I leave her, crying and wailing in misery. Arise, Romeo. Stand up, if you have any manliness in you. For your lady's sake, do not give way so abjectly. Why should you be in such deep despair?

Romeo: Nurse!

Nurse: Alas! Signior Romeo! Well, we shall all die some day, then our troubles will be over!

Romeo: What news have you of my lady? How is she? Does she not look upon me as a practised murderer, seeing that, at the very beginning of our happiness, I have shed the blood of one so near to her? Tell me how she is, and what she says, and what she thinks of our love, so soon broken!

Nurse: She does not refer to it, but spends her time in weeping. Sometimes, she casts herself down on her couch and, then, springing up, she utters Tybalt's name. Then she calls on Romeo, throwing herself down, weeps again.

Romeo: As though the sound of that unlucky name had killed her, as surely as by a bullet from a gun, levelled with fatal aim. Just as the wicked hand, belonging to that name, killed her cousin. Say, good father, say if you know what portion of my worthless frame harbors that odious name of mine, that I may lay waste its detested dwelling place!

[*Drawing his sword.*]

Friar Laurence: Stop! Commit no such mad act of rashness! Though by your form you appear to be a man, yet you weep like a woman, and your reckless actions are more like those of a wild animal, than of a rational human being. Weak, effeminate conduct is unbecoming in a man, or, even were you woman, as you are man, the unreasoning conduct of a beast would not suit you! I am surprised at your behavior. By St. Francis, I did not consider that you were of so weak a character. Because you have killed a Capulet, will you follow that up by killing yourself? Would that improve matters? Would it not be the death of the lady Juliet, too, if you committed such an accursed deed upon your own body, seeing that her life is bound up in yours? It is foolish to curse the day of your birth, the earth and the skies, for all these things go into the fashioning of a man, and therefore have part in you. You would throw all away at one sweep, were you to commit that deed you contemplate.

For shame! You disgrace your sex, your love and your intelligence. You possess them all in plenty, yet, like a miser, instead of using them as you ought, you turn them quite away from their legitimate purposes, which are to adorn your sex, your love and your intelligence. That shapely form of yours is no better than a moulded figure of wax, if you forsake the courage that a man should have. The vows of deepest affection, which you have uttered, become a mockery and a falsehood, for how can you keep your vow to cherish your dear love, if you slay yourself? And your good sense, which ought to adorn your manly figure and your faithful love and which so well suits them, seems to have greatly altered, playing you false in the guidance of your affairs and, so, proving rather a source of danger than of safety. Just as gunpowder, carried by an unpractised hand, is liable to be set aflame by unskilful handling, and the unlucky soldier is blown to pieces by what should have been the safeguard of his life. Courage, man!

Do not despair! Your lady, for whom you have run the risk of death, is still living, you are blessed in that. And you, yourself, have escaped death at the hand of Tybalt, whom you killed instead of being slain by him; you are blessed in that. And, again, you were in danger of death by the operation of the law, as a punishment for your fault. That death sentence has been commuted to banishment. Once again, you have cause for rejoicing. A whole shower of blessings rains down upon you, good fortune comes to seek you with smiling face, but you, like a sulky, rude girl, turn a discontented face toward both your happiness and your good luck. Beware! Such ingratitude brings people to an unhappy end.

Go to your lady, as you had arranged. Begone to her home, and console her with your company for a while, but beware of lingering until the sentries are posted for the night, for then it will be impossible to leave the city. You must make your way to Mantua, and take up your abode there, until it shall be safe to make your marriage known. Then we shall try to persuade your families to forget their differences, and obtain for you the prince's forgiveness. Until, at last, you return with untold happiness, much more by far than this sorrow that has befallen you now. Nurse, return to your lady first, and give her my good wishes. Tell her to try, if possible, to see that everyone in the house retires early. They will be the more likely to do this, on account of their mourning for Tybalt. And say that Romeo will follow you.

Nurse: I vow to heaven, I would have been satisfied to remain here for hours, listening to such good advice. How wonderful it is to be so learned! Signior Romeo, I will tell my mistress you are coming.

Romeo: Yes, do, and tell her that she may get ready to scold me!

Nurse: My lady sent you this ring, young man. I hope you hasten, for the hour is no longer early.

[*Exit.*]

Romeo: How this has re-awakened my happiness!

Friar Laurence: Farewell, you must now depart. This is your position—you must either leave the city before the sentries are posted for the night, or you must go immediately when they leave their posts, at dawn, when it will be necessary for you to disguise yourself. Stay in Mantua, and I shall seek out your servant, and send by him all the news of this city, in whatever concerns yourself. He shall tell you of whatever good fortune may chance for you, as often as I can send to you. The hour is late, you must go hence. Adieu!

Romeo: I would hate to take leave of you so hurriedly, if it were not that a bliss beyond words is awaiting me. Adieu!

[*Exit.*]

ACT III · SCENE 4

[*A room in Capulet's house.*]
[*Enter Capulet, Lady Capulet and Paris.*]

Capulet: Events have happened so very unfortunately that I have not had an opportunity to influence my daughter in your favor yet. You see, young man, she had a great affection for her cousin, Tybalt, as, indeed, I myself had also. Alas! The end must come to us all, it is our destiny! The night is too far advanced to expect Juliet to come from her chamber again. Indeed, I myself should have retired some time ago had you not been here.

Paris: These days of sorrow are scarcely days of courtship. I will take my leave, madam, pray give your daughter my good wishes.

Lady Capulet: I will do so, and, in the morning, I will try to find out her feelings toward you. She is too full of sorrow tonight, and is remaining in her chamber.

Capulet: I think, young man, that I may give you an absolute promise that Juliet will accept your suit. I believe that she will allow me to guide her in every way. Indeed, I am sure of it. Seek her out now, madam, before you retire to rest. Tell her of Count Paris' suit, and say that on Wednesday next—but, wait a moment! What day is this?

Paris: Monday, my lord.

Capulet: Indeed! Monday! Then Wednesday will be too short a time; we will have it on Thursday—say that on Thursday she shall wed the count. Will that day be too soon for you, count? Or does such an early date displease you? There will be no great feast. We shall invite a very small company, on account of the recent death of Tybalt. For, if we have great rejoicings, the world will think that we held him in small estimation, as he is so near a relative. For that reason, we will have but a very few guests, and that will be all. Do you agree to have the marriage on Thursday?

Paris: Sir, I heartily wish that Thursday were tomorrow!

Capulet: Farewell, then, and let it be settled for Thursday. Madam, seek our daughter's room at once, before you reitre, and let her know that her marriage has been arranged. Adieu, young man. Bring lights for me to go to my room! By my soul, the night is so nearly over that it will shortly be morning. Farewell!

[*Exit.*]

ACT III · SCENE 5

[*Juliet's chamber.*]

[*Enter Romeo and Juliet.*]

Juliet: Must you go? It is far from daybreak yet! Those notes you heard, which so dismayed you, were not those of the lark, singing at the advent of the day, but those of the nightingale, singing her evening song. She sits, each night, upon the bough of the pomegranate tree, and fills the air with music. It was the nightingale, dearest, I am sure.

Romeo: Nay, it was not the nightingale's song, but the morning carol of the lark, the forerunner of day. And see, beloved, how in the eastern sky, the clouds of the night are pierced and fretted by growing lines of light. The starry lamps of heaven are faded and dim, and, upon the summit of the vapor-circled hills, stands joyous morning, with outspread wings, ready and poised for flight. Now I must make my choice, and must either remain here, and lose my life, or bid you farewell, and save it.

Juliet: It is not the dawn you see, I swear. It is some shooting star, some passing radiance sent out by the sun to shine upon your path to Mantua. Therefore, as dawn is not yet breaking, stay awhile.

Romeo: I will remain, and willingly give my life for your delight. I have no other wish if you desire it so. I agree that those faint streaks of light are not the growing dawn, but only the white reflection from the face of Diana, and that clear song, vibrating in the lofty arch of heaven, is not the lark's, but that of some other bird. My desire to remain here is much greater than my resolution to leave you. Therefore, since death is the penalty, I will meet it happily, for my love desires me to stay. How are you, my sweet? Come, converse with me, night is not over yet.

Juliet: Oh yes! Is it over, and you must hasten away! Go quickly! It is the lark's song that sounds so unpleasing in our ears. No longer do its tones seem sweet and mellow, but discordant and tuneless, bringing the unwelcome news that we must part. The lark's trills or phrases, called divisions, are supposed to be very sweet. I do not find the division she makes between us two to be sweet! It is said that the hateful toad has changed eyes with the lark. I wish they had changed voices also, for the lark's voice now parts us from each other's embraces with dismay, and chases my love far from me, as though its music were a hunting song at dawn! Oh, go at once! Hasten! The dawn grows brighter!

Romeo: Does it grow brighter? Nay, our sorrows grow darker still!

[*Enter Nurse.*]

Nurse: My lady!

Juliet: Yes?

Nurse: Madam, your mother is coming to your room to see you. It is daybreak now, be on your guard! Watch carefully.

[*Exit.*]

Juliet: Then through this open window daylight must enter, and you, my soul, must go out.

Romeo: Adieu, beloved! Kiss me once more, and I will leave you.

[*Descends.*]

Juliet: Have you really gone? My love! My lord! My friend! You must send me tidings every day, of all the hours we shall be parted, for every moment will seem like many days! Oh, how much older I shall be, by this manner of reckoning, before my love and I can meet again!

Romeo: Adieu! I will send you tidings, without fail, at every opportunity that presents itself.

Juliet: Oh! Shall we ever see each other more?

Romeo: Never think of doubting it! And, in future days, we shall often pass pleasant hours in recalling these times of danger and sorrow.

Juliet: O heaven! My heart foretells disaster! Now that you have reached the ground, I seem to look down upon you as one looks into the grave of a friend. And, if my eyes still see properly, your face is pale!

Romeo: You look pale also to my eyes, believe me, dearest. Grief steals the warm blood from our cheeks. Farewell! Farewell!

[*Exit.*]

Juliet: It is said by all that fortune is capricious and changeful. If that be so, then why does fortune assault Romeo, who is so steadfast? Why should capricious fortune accompany him? Yet, let her be capricious. Then, there is hope that she will change her mind, and separate him from me no longer.

Lady Capulet: [*Within.*] Juliet! Have you risen yet?

Juliet: Who is that speaking? Is it my lady mother? Surely, she is very late in retiring, or very early in rising? Some unusual reason must have brought her here!

[*Enter Lady Capulet.*]

Lady Capulet: How is my daughter?

Juliet: I feel ill, madam.

Lady Capulet: Are you still shedding tears for the death of Tybalt? Do you think those floods of tears will sweep him out of his tomb! And, even if that were possible, he would not be living. Therefore, cease your weeping. To sorrow for the death of a friend is a sign of affection, but to carry that sorrow to excess is foolishness.

Juliet: Do not forbid me to mourn for such a heartfelt loss.

Lady Capulet: But in doing so, you feel the bitterness of the loss, but still cannot have the lost one.

Juliet: Yet, as my heart is so heavy with grief, it is impossible for me not to mourn for the one who is the cause of it.

Lady Capulet: I think, however, that your sorrow arises less from the loss of Tybalt, than from the escape of the scoundrel who slew him, my daughter.

Juliet: To whom, madam, do you refer?

Lady Capulet: The scoundrel Romeo.

Juliet: Romeo can hardly be called a "scoundrel." May heaven forgive him! From my soul, I pardon him also. Nevertheless, he has caused me more sorrow than any other man in the world!

Lady Capulet: You grieve because the treacherous murderer is still alive?

Juliet: Yes, mother, and beyond the reach of my arms! I wish that I, and only I, were appointed to avenge the death of Tybalt!

Lady Capulet: Do not be afraid that his death will not be avenged. Therefore, cease your tears. There is someone in Mantua, where that young exiled criminal has taken up his residence, who will, at my request, give him a drink that will send him, in a very short time, to join his victim. When this is accomplished, I trust your griefs will cease.

Juliet: It is certain that Romeo will be always in my thoughts, until I know him to be dead—so filled is my heart with sadness for my cousin's death. If you succeed, lady, in finding a messenger whom you can send to Mantua with that deadly drink, I would so add to the mixture, that I promise you Romeo should soon be laid down in peace, when he had received it. Oh, it grieves me to the soul to hear his name, knowing that I may not seek him—to avenge the death of my kinsman upon the person of his murderer!

Lady Capulet: If you will do your part, I promise to find a messenger. But, for the present, I have some glad news to give you, my daughter.

Juliet: And right thankful are we to hear glad news at this unhappy time. Tell me your tidings, I pray you.

Lady Capulet: Truly, you have a most excellent father, Juliet. To divert your thoughts from your grief, he has arranged an unexpected day of happiness for you, which neither you nor I had anticipated.

Juliet: And what is that fortunate day, madam?

Lady Capulet: Well, my daughter, on next Thursday morning, you are to be happily married to the brave and handsome young nobleman, Count Paris, at St. Peter's Church.

Juliet: What! Marry Paris at St. Peter's Church! I declare I will not! Such haste is most amazing! My marriage is arranged before the would-be bridegroom has even presented himself as a suitor! I beg you, lady, let my father know that I do not wish to wed so soon. Even were I considering the question, my choice would sooner fall on Romeo—who is hateful to me, as you know—than on Count Paris. Truly! You have brought me tidings indeed!

Lady Capulet: Your father is approaching. Acquaint him with your decision, and see what he will say.

[*Enter Capulet and Nurse.*]

Capulet: Dew generally falls after the sun has gone down, but here, it seems to be actually raining after the setting of Tybalt's sun. What is the matter, daughter? You are like a waterfall! You seem to be always weeping! You are like the ocean, a vessel and a breeze all in one: your eyes, like the sea, are alternately ebbing and flowing with water; you, yourself, may be compared to the vessel, floating on this briny sea; your sighs are like the gales that sweep over the ocean. Those gales, together with such floods of tears, will bring you to shipwreck, unless you stop them, and cease your lamentations. Well, madam, have you told our daughter what we have decided?

Lady Capulet: Yes, my lord. She is greatly obliged to you, but she declines to think of it. I wish the crazy girl were dead!

Capulet: Wait a moment! Let me understand you, madam. Do you mean to say that she refuses? Is she not filled with gratitude for the trouble we have taken on her account? And with pride, at the excellent marriage we have arranged? Is she not happy to hear that our efforts on her behalf have secured for her such an honorable and desirable husband?

Juliet: I cannot take any pride in what you have done, because I could not be proud of a thing, which is so utterly distasteful to me. But I am grateful for it, as you did it out of love for me, and your intentions were kind.

Capulet: Indeed! Hairsplitter! Learned logician! What is all this lawyerlike argument about? You cannot take pride in it—and you are grateful—and you decline—and you accept! Saucy young madam! Let me hear no more talk of grateful or ungrateful, proud or not proud, but get your precious self ready to accompany Count Paris next Thursday to the church, or you shall be carried there by force. Shame on you, you pale creature! You saucy miss!

Lady Capulet: For shame! Have you taken leave of your senses?

Juliet: I beg of you, dear father, to listen to me for a moment. See, I kneel before you!

Capulet: Away, you saucy creature! Listen to me! Either you are married on Thursday, or you never see me again. It is no use making any objections, so do not attempt it! I can scarcely keep my hands from you! We thought, madam, that we should have been happier, had Heaven granted us more children than this only one. I see that we should have been happier in having none at all, for she brings nothing but sorrow upon us. Shame on her, worthless creature!

Nurse: The blessings of Heaven on her! It is not right of you, my lord, to scold her thus.

Capulet: Indeed, madam wisdom! Why so? Say no more. Go and talk with your friends.

Nurse: I am saying no harm of anyone. I am not disrespectful.

Capulet: Oh, go away!

Nurse: Am I forbidden to use my tongue?

Capulet: Silence, you foolish mutterer! Go and entertain your companions with your wisdom, as you drink together. We can do without it here!

Lady Capulet: Calm yourself, my lord.

Capulet: By the mass! It is enough to put anyone into a frenzy. Early and late, busy or at leisure, in solitude or among friends, I have always worked with one object in view, namely, the arranging of a suitable marriage for my daughter. And now, when all is satisfactorily settled, and a young man of high rank and excellent training, with wide estates, and all the virtues one man may have, besides being as handsome a youth as one could imagine as one's ideal, is willing and anxious to make her his bride, conceive how it annoys and disappoints me to hear a miserable whining creature, a whimpering doll, at the moment when such good fortune is offering itself to her, saying she cannot marry, she has no affection for the man, she is not old enough to wed and she craves my forgiveness.

But if you refuse to marry the count, all the forgiveness you will get from me will be permission to go and seek your living wherever you like, for you will no longer find a home here. See that you consider this carefully, for it is not my custom to say things in jest. There is not much time, so take counsel and be wise. If you are my daughter, you will marry the count. If you are not, then I do not care what becomes of you. I will cast you off altogether, and not a penny of my wealth shall you inherit. Consider it carefully, for I mean what I say, and I shall not break my word.

[*Exit.*]

Juliet: Will Heaven have no compassion on me, in my deep sorrow? Dearest mother, help me! Put off this wedding for awhile, even for a few days. Or let me die, and make my bridal couch in the dark tomb where my cousin sleeps.

Lady Capulet: I will not say a single word on your behalf, so do not ask me. You may do whatever you choose. I will have nothing more to do with you!

[*Exit.*]

Juliet: Oh, heaven! What can I do, Nurse, to avoid this marriage? My husband, whom I love, is on earth. My God, in whom I trust, is in heaven. But how can I trust that He will overrule these earthly trials, except by having faith sent me from heaven, even by Romeo, if he were there? But to do that, he must leave this world! Oh help me, and reassure me. Alas! What have I done that fate should be so unkind? What do you think, Nurse? Can you say nothing to cheer me? Give me some hope.

Nurse: Then, truly, this is what I say! Your husband is in exile, and the chances are hopelessly against his ever returning to claim you as his wife. Even if he should come, it would have to be in secret. That being so, I should advise you to agree to this wedding, and become the count's wife. He is most handsome, and his eyes are as fine, alert and piercing as an eagle's. Romeo is not to be compared to him. Upon my soul, I think you are most fortunate to have this second marriage offered to you. It greatly surpasses the former one. Even if it did not, your first husband is dead, or as good as dead, for he is equally lost to you. He might as well be dead, as separated from you in the way he is at present.

Juliet: Do you really mean this?

Nurse: I'll be hanged if there's anything else to be done.

Juliet: I hope you will be, then.

Nurse: What do you say?

Juliet: Well, you have truly consoled me. Now go to my mother, and say that I have gone to the good priest's cell to beg forgiveness and to get absolution for having offended my father.

Nurse: Indeed I will, and I think you are right to do so.

[*Exit.*]

Juliet: The wicked old devil! I scarcely know which is worse—wishing me to perjure myself thus, in swearing false marriage vows, or to criticize my beloved, with the same tongue with which she has so often praised him above all others! Away, wise adviser! Never more shall you know the thoughts of my heart! I will hasten to the priest, and ask if he has any plan to help me. Should no one be able to aid me, I can, at least, die.

[*Exit.*]

ACT IV · SCENE 1

[*Verona. Friar Laurence's cell.*]

[*Enter Friar Laurence and Paris.*]

Friar Laurence: It is fixed for an early date, if, as you say, my son, the wedding is to take place on Thursday.

Paris: My bride's parents wish it to take place on that day, and I am not so slow in love, that I should wish for any delay.

Friar Laurence: It is most unusual to arrange a marriage before the suitor knows whether the lady will consent. You say you have not yet courted her. I disapprove greatly of such a course of action.

Paris: I have not yet spoken much of love, for the lady Juliet is overwhelmed with grief for her cousin's death, and courting would seem out of place in a house of mourning. But Lord Capulet, very wisely I think, feels that her abandonment to such grief may have an exceedingly ill effect upon her, and do her much harm. He therefore wishes our marriage to take place at an earlier date than would otherwise have been thought of, in order to divert the lady's thoughts from her grief, and to encourage her to forget, in the company of others, what she is too much inclined to brood over, when alone. Here, then, you have the reason for such a speedy marriage.

Friar Laurence: [*Aside.*] I wish I did not know of a reason why it should be delayed. Look, my son, the lady Juliet is approaching.

[*Enter Juliet.*]

Paris: A fortunate meeting, my lady and my wife!

Juliet: Perhaps so, sir, when I am wedded to you.

Paris: That perhaps will be a certainty next Thursday.

Juliet: What is to happen, will happen!

Friar Laurence: That is quite true.

Paris: Have you come to confess to Friar Laurence?

Juliet: If I reply to that, I shall be making confession to you.

Paris: When you tell him of yourself, do not say that you have no affection for me.

Juliet: I can say to you that I have a great affection for him.

Paris: And I believe and hope that you have the same for me.

Juliet: If I tell the good father that, the declaration will have much more value, being given in your absence, than it would have, were I to say so now, in front of you.

Paris: It grieves me to see your face so disfigured by weeping.

Juliet: The tears have little to boast of, for my face was not beautiful, even before they began their malicious work.

Paris: Now you are more unjust to it than even the tears, when you speak so.

Juliet: It is not injustice to speak the truth, and I said what I thought to my face!

Paris: Your face belongs to me, and you have uttered lies against what is mine.

Juliet: You may be right, for my face is indeed not my own.

Good priest, are you at liberty to hear my confession now, or will it be better that I should see you at the evening service?

Friar Laurence: I am at liberty now, my sorrowful child. May we beg that you leave us, Count Paris?

Paris: Heaven forbid that I should hinder your prayers! I shall wake you early on Thursday, lady. Farewell, until that morning, one parting caress!

[*Exit.*]

Juliet: O father, come and join your tears with mine, when you have locked your door against all intruders. My sorrows are beyond man's aid. I am hopeless and despairing!

Friar Laurence: I know, my daughter, before you tell me, how great your sorrows are, and I am almost distracted for your sake. I am told that on next Thursday you must wed Count Paris, and that there is no hope of delay.

Juliet: Oh, do not remind me of it, unless at the same time, you say that you have found a remedy. If you, with all your learning and wit, cannot aid me in the matter, I will, without hesitation, aid myself to freedom with this knife, if only you will give the deed sanction. Heaven inspired our love, and you united us in wedlock. This weapon shall end both, before I contract another marriage. Therefore, good father, give me your advice quickly, out of the accumulated wisdom of your age and experience. For if you cannot, this cruel knife shall decide in my extremity, between me and my perplexities, and determine the outcome of this affair, from which all the authority of your long life and experience is unable to rescue me with honor. Speak quickly. But, if what you have to say does not tell me of a cure for my woes, I am ready and willing to give up my life.

Friar Laurence: Wait, my child. I see a faint hope of escape for you. It demands, to carry it through, a courage as daring as the situation is desperate, from which it will set you free. If your courage is equal to the task of slaying yourself rather than wed the count, then it is more than probable you will dare an adventure which is almost the same as death, in order to avoid the dishonor of a double marriage. Especially as you are willing to encounter the reality of death for that reason. So I will help you to a way of escape, if your courage is equal to it.

Juliet: You cannot ask me anything I will not do, in order to avoid this marriage. Command me to spring from the top turret of this building, or wander in the haunts of thieves and robbers, or hide in caves and dens among crawling serpents or fierce bears, or go at night into a sepulchre, strewn with the bones of corpses rotting in their tomb, and with fleshless skulls lying around or tell me I must conceal myself in a newly dug grave, and lie there by a shrouded corpse. Command me to do any of these things, which only to hear about would, at one time, have thrilled me with horror, and it shall not make me fear or tremble, if thereby I may escape this fate, and keep my wifely vows unbroken.

Friar Laurence: Have patience, then, and listen. Return home with a cheerful expression, and put away your grief. Tell your parents that you are willing to marry the count, and tomorrow night, which is Wednesday, arrange to sleep alone. Do not even have your nurse in the room. Then, take this small bottle of distilled liquor, which I now give you, and, as soon as you are in bed, drink its contents. In a few moments, a feeling of weakness will pervade all your body, your blood will run cold and chill, your pulse will cease its usual course, and beat no longer, your limbs will be cold, and no one will be able to say, "she breathes." Your cheeks and lips will lose their color, your eyes will close as if in death and the whole of your body, no longer supple and pliant, and under control of the will, will become cold and rigid. For 40 hours and more you will remain, to all appearance, dead, pinched and pale. Then, you will awaken, without feeling any ill effects, as though you had merely been roused from peaceful and tranquil slumber.

On the wedding morning, when your lover comes to

wake you, they will find you, to all appearance, dead. You will shortly afterward be carried, according to our national custom, richly dressed in your finest garments, on an open platform to your family burial place, where all your kinsfolk are entombed. During the interval between this and your awakening, I shall send a message to Romeo, telling him of our plan, and, by the time you awaken, he will be here, and he and I together will come and await the time when the effect of the drug passes off. He will then carry you off immediately to Mantua. This is my plan to extricate you from this dishonorable marriage, unless some sudden whim or feminine timidity saps your courage in carrying it out.

Juliet: Let me have it! Be sure that nothing shall lessen my courage, or make me afraid.

Friar Laurence: Here! Go now, and may you be valiant and successful in your task. Meanwhile, I shall send a swift messenger to take the news to your husband in Mantua.

Juliet: Affection will strengthen me, and that strength will enable me to succeed. Adieu, good father!

[*Exit.*]

ACT IV · SCENE 2

[*A large room in Capulet's house.*]

[*Enter Capulet, Lady Capulet, Nurse and servants.*]

Capulet: Ask the people whose names are written here to come to our wedding feast. [*Exit servant.*] You, fellow, go and find me twenty skilful cooks, and hire them.

Second Servant: You shall have no unskilful ones, my lord. I shall test them by seeing whether they can lick their fingers.

Capulet: How can you test them in that way?

Second Servant: Well, sir, a cook who could not lick his own fingers must be a very poor one, therefore I will have nothing to do with him.

Capulet: Well, be off! [*Exit second servant.*] We are very far from being sufficiently prepared for this event. Has Juliet gone to the friar's cell?

Nurse: Yes, indeed, she has.

Capulet: Well, I hope she will benefit by his advice, the discontented, obstinate little baggage!

[*Enter Juliet.*]

Nurse: Here she is, returning from her confession with actually a smiling face.

Capulet: Well, my stubborn lady, where have you been wandering?

Juliet: Where I have been taught the wrongfulness of my resistance to your commands. I have been asked by the good priest to kneel and ask your forgiveness. I pray you, pardon me! From this time forward, I shall be guided entirely by your wishes.

Capulet: Let some messenger go and seek Count Paris, and tell him the news. I will arrange that they be married tomorrow morning.

Juliet: I saw the young count when I was with Friar Laurence, and showed him such suitable marks of affection as I could without seeming too bold.

Capulet: You please me greatly, you have done rightly. Do not kneel any longer. You have behaved very well indeed. I must see Count Paris. Yes, indeed, send for him at once, bring him here. By Heaven, this good priest has laid us all under great obligation to him!

Juliet: Come with me, Nurse, into my chamber, and help me to seek out and arrange what finery will be necessary, that I may be suitably dressed tomorrow.

Lady Capulet: There is no need to hurry. The wedding is not to be tomorrow, but on Thursday.

Capulet: Yes, accompany her, Nurse. The wedding shall be tomorrow.

[*Exit Juliet and Nurse.*]

Lady Capulet: Our preparations will not be complete, and it is late now.

Capulet: Nonsense! I will go round and hurry on the work, and we shall be ready in time, I am sure. You go and help dress the bride, and leave me to see to the rest. I shall not go to rest tonight, but, for once, will perform a housewife's duties. Hey there! There is no one in! No matter! I shall take the news to the young count myself, and ask him to be ready in the morning. I am in wondrously good spirits, since that stubborn child of mine has been brought back to a sense of her duty.

[*Exit.*]

ACT IV · SCENE 3

[Juliet's chamber.]

[Enter Juliet and Nurse.]

Juliet: Yes, I think those robes are most suitable. I beg you, kind Nurse, to let me be alone tonight. I must offer up many prayers to implore Heaven to look mercifully down upon me, for you know how much I need it.

[Enter Lady Capulet.]

Lady Capulet: Hello there, daughter. Have you much to do? Are you in need of assistance?

Juliet: I need nothing, madam. We have gathered together all that is required for tomorrow, and suitable to the occasion. Now I should like you to leave me. Take Nurse to help you in your preparations, for I can well believe you must have almost more to do than you can accomplish in the little time at your disposal.

Lady Capulet: Good night! Retire to rest at once for you will require all your strength tomorrow.

[Exit Lady Capulet and Nurse.]

Juliet: Adieu! Heaven alone can tell whether we shall ever see each other again. I am sick with dread! An icy fear seems to grip me, chilling my very blood! I will recall them, to revive my fainting courage. Nurse! Of what use would she be to me in my desperate venture? I must go through my dreary task unaided.

Now, to take the potion! But suppose it does not have the desired effect! Must I then wed Count Paris in the morning? Never! This dagger will prevent that necessity. Let it remain here, ready to my hand.

[Laying down a dagger.]

Suppose this mixture should be a poison which the friar has cunningly contrived that I shall take, in case inquiries are made on my refusal to marry Count Paris, and the friar be disgraced on account of my marriage to Romeo, which he performed. It may chance to be so, there is a risk, but I will not believe it, for his goodness and honor have been often proved before now. What shall I do if, after I have been placed in the vault, I waken before my love arrives to save me? How terrifying is the thought! I shall run the risk of being choked by foul air in that horrible place, into which no wholesome life-giving air can find its way, and, before Romeo can reach me, I shall be dead.

Even if I do not die by the poisoned air, it is more probable that the dreadful thoughts which will be forced upon my mind by that place of death, and by the fact that I am there alone, at dead of night, in a tomb which has received the bodies of dead Capulets for centuries, where my cousin's body, gory with his wound, and scarcely cold in his tomb, also lies rotting in his winding sheet, and where it is said that ghosts are frequently seen at certain hours of the night—it is very probable that if I waken before Romeo comes, what with the terror of those thoughts, the hideous scents and sights, and the sound of ghastly shrieks and groans, such as mandrakes are said to utter, and which cause the unhappy hearers to lose their senses, surrounded with all these terrors, shall I not go raving mad, and begin insanely to make playthings of the dead man's bones, and, perhaps, strip my cousin's wounded corpse of its funeral clothes, or, in my frenzy, dash out my brains, using as a weapon the bone of some dead ancestor? See! I almost imagine I behold dead Tybalt's spirit arising to revenge itself on my husband, whose sword it was that ran him through the body! Stop, Tybalt! Hold! I am coming, Romeo! This drink will bring me to thy arms!

[*She falls upon her bed, within the curtains.*]

ACT IV · SCENE 4

[*Capulet's audience room.*]

[*Enter Lady Capulet and Nurse.*]

Lady Capulet: Wait, Nurse, here are my keys. Bring more spices.

Nurse: They need more dates and apples in the room where the pies are made.

[*Enter Capulet.*]

Capulet: Now, hurry! Hurry! Move about quickly. The cock has crowed a second time, and the morning bell has rung—it is three o'clock. Good Angelica, see that the baked meats are all prepared, and do not let anything be missing because of its costliness. Provide a generous feast for all.

Nurse: Leave these matters to others, housewife, and go to your chamber. Truly you will be ill tomorrow, after being awake all night.

Capulet: Not in the least. On my word! I have been up all night before this, and without such good reason, yet have not felt any ill effects.

Lady Capulet: Yes, you have been after other game in your younger days. But I will see to it now that you have no more such wakeful nights.

[*Exit Lady Capulet and Nurse.*]

Capulet: Oh! Jealousy, is it? Jealousy?

[*Enter three or four servants with spits, logs and basket.*]

Here, you sir! What's that you've got?

First Servant: I do not know, sir, but the cook wants them.

Capulet: Well, get along then! [*Exit first servant.*] You, knave, bring more logs, drier than these. You can learn where they are from Peter.

Second Servant: I can find out where they are by my own wits, without disturbing Peter to tell me. I have a head on my shoulders.

[*Exit.*]

Capulet: By the mass, a good answer. That is a jolly rascal, he shall be head "logger" man. On my word, day is breaking already. We shall hear the count, with his musicians, immediately. He promised he would arrive early. [*Music within.*] There he is, coming now! Nurse! Wife! Hallo! Why, Nurse! [*Re-enter Nurse.*] Go and wake your mistress, and adorn her for her wedding. I will converse with the bridegroom meanwhile. Come, hasten! Count Paris is already here. Hurry!

[*Exit.*]

ACT IV · SCENE 5

[*Juliet's chamber. Juliet on the bed.*]

[*Enter Nurse.*]

Nurse: Madam! My lady! Juliet! Sound asleep, I swear. Come, love! Why, lady! For shame, lazy one! Dear one, wake up! Madam! Come, darling! Why, bride! How is this? No reply? You are making up for the time you will lose after this, are you? And you mean to take all the slumber you can get. You will not sleep so soundly after your wedding—Heaven bless me! By the Virgin, how fast asleep she lies! I shall be obliged to rouse her, however. Lady! Juliet! Yes, you will let your bridegroom catch you sleeping. That would startle you out of bed, I vow! Will she never waken! Why, she has been up, and has dressed herself and lain down once more! I really must rouse her. Madam! Lady! Oh, me! What is here? Help, help! My mistress is dead! Alas! That I have ever lived to see this day! Bring brandy, help! My master! My mistress!

[*Enter Lady Capulet.*]

Lady Capulet: What is all this clamor?

Nurse: Oh, unhappy day!

Lady Capulet: What has happened?

Nurse: See! See what lies there. Oh, miserable day!

Lady Capulet: Alas! Alas! My daughter, the light of my existence, wake! Open your eyes, recover, or I shall die too! Help! Help! Call for help, Nurse!

[*Enter Capulet.*]

Capulet: Goodness! Why is Juliet taking so long? Fetch her out at once, her bridegroom is here.

Nurse: She is dead! She is dead! Alas, she lives no longer.

Lady Capulet: O woeful day! She is gone! She's dead! She's dead!

Capulet: What! Let me look. Alas! Alas! The chill of death is upon her, her blood no longer flows, her limbs are rigid. The life has long left these cold lips. Chill death has descended upon her as an untimely frost nips and destroys the fairest blossom of the garden.

Nurse: Oh, miserable day!

Lady Capulet: Oh, sorrowful time!

Capulet: Death, snatching my child away, and leaving me to mourn, has taken from me the power of expressing my grief: words fail me.

[*Enter Friar Laurence and Paris, with musicians.*]

Friar Laurence: Come, is the bride ready to go to church?

Capulet: Yes, ready to go there, but she will never come back again.

O, my son, Paris! A grim bridegroom has been before you. That fair blossom, your betrothed, has mated with death on her marriage evening. Now I have no successor, no heir but death. He has taken my child and, in taking her, robbed me of all. Life and wealth are nothing to me. He may take my life also, and I will leave all to him, since he has made them worthless.

Paris: Long and eagerly have I looked for the dawning of this day, and now that it has come, what a spectacle greets my unhappy gaze!

Lady Capulet: O what a miserable, sorrowful and piteous day! The most melancholy moment ever reached by Time in the endless, toilsome years of his long journey! We had only one child, a single one was all that fate gave to us. One to bestow her love upon us, to cheer our hearts and be a comfort to us, and that one is snatched away by the ruthless hand of death!

Nurse: O misery! O wretched day! The most doleful, pitiable day that I ever saw! Never has there been such a day of gloom! O doleful day!

Paris: O hateful death, thou hast deceived and cheated us. Thy cruelty has separated us forever, injured and killed my love, and quite crushed us! O my beloved! My life, nay, no longer my life, but still my beloved, even in death.

Capulet: Treated by fate with contempt, afflicted, sacrificed and slain! Oh, why has such affliction visited us at the moment when all seemed well, and killed our joy when all were preparing for such a happy ceremony? O my daughter! My heart of hearts, is it true that thou art slain? Alas! It is true, and life holds nothing for me now but misery!

Friar Laurence: Calm yourselves! Be tranquil! You will never remedy your sorrows by such wild outbursts of sorrow! You shared with Heaven the possession of this sweet and lovely child. Now she belongs entirely to Heaven, and that is the maiden's gain. It was beyond your power, though you shared in her possession, to keep her alive, but Heaven can keep the spiritual part of her in everlasting life. You worked untiringly for her advancement and her gain, for that was your greatest joy. Why should you now mourn, when she has gained the heights of Paradise? It would seem to show that you did not love your child truly and unselfishly, when your sorrow is so wild, although she is now happy. Her lot is the happier one, to be loved and yet die young, rather than to be loved and endure the trials of a long life. Then weep no longer, but strew this lovely maid's body with sweet flowers and, according to our national custom, carry her to the church, clothed in her richest garments. If you think properly of her death, you will see that reason urges us to rejoice for her sake, although our natural feelings of love and affection would lead us to sorrow deeply for our loss.

Capulet: All the joyous preparations we made for the celebration of a wedding feast must now be employed in the service of death and burial! The happy music gives place to the tolling of solemn knells. The marriage feast will become a melancholy funeral meal and, instead of stately anthems, we shall hear the sound of mournful funeral chants. The fair blossoms that were to adorn a bride must now decorate a coffin. All is changed, and everything must serve a purpose opposite to that for which it was prepared.

Friar Laurence: Retire into your chamber, my lord, and you, Lady Capulet, accompany him. Come also, count. Let us all make ready to perform the funeral rites of this sweet maiden. The powers above frown upon you, on account of some wrong which they see. Do not tempt their anger further by rebelling against their decree.

[*Exit Capulet, Lady Capulet, Paris and Friar Laurence.*]

First Musician: There is nothing left for us to do, I'll swear, but to put our instruments in their cases, and take our leave.

Nurse: Worthy fellows, yes, indeed, put them away, for I am sure you see that the case is a very sad one.

[*Exit.*]

First Musician: Yes, truly, this case might be a better one!

[*Enter Peter.*]

Peter: Good fellows, play "Heart's ease" for me, unless you wish to see me die!

First Musician: Why do you want that tune?

Peter: Because, musicians, my heart is beating to the tune of a sorrowful ditty. So play me a joyful one to lighten it.

First Musician: Not a note will we play. You can see, yourself, that it would be out of place.

Peter: You refuse?

First Musician: Yes.

Peter: Then I will let you have it, without fail.

First Musician: What will you let us have?

Peter: Not payment, certainly. All you will get from me will be mockery. I will give you the "musician"!

First Musician: Then you will get the "servant" from me!

Peter: Then the "servant" will lay his knife about your head. I will put up with none of your fancies. I'll *re* you, I'll *fa* you! Do you note me?

First Musician: If you *re* us, and *fa* us, it is you who will do the noting.

Second Musician: Put away that knife, I beg you, and let us hear some of your wisdom!

Peter: Then, here goes, to assault you with my wisdom! I will sheathe my knife, but my wit shall be my weapon. Tell me this, bravely:

> When biting sorrows pierce the breast,
> And melancholy keeps from rest
> The silver tones of music cheer,

Now, why does the rhyme say "silver tones," with reference to music? I will ask you first, Simon Catling.

First Musician: Well, sir, because music and silver both sound sweetly.

Peter: Very good. What is your opinion, Hugh Rebeck?

Second Musician: I should think it is because we play for silver.

Peter: Very good also. What do you think, James Soundpost?

Third Musician: I am sure I can't say.

Peter: Oh, pardon me! You are the singer. I will answer for you, then. It says "the silver tones of music," because musicians do not usually get gold for their playing!

> The silver tones of music cheer,
> Revive the spirits, and banish fear.

[*Exit.*]

First Musician: Tiresome fellow!

Second Musician: Let him go hang, saucy Jack! Let us go in and wait for the funeral. We can then remain for the feast!

[*Exit.*]

ACT V · SCENE 1

[*Mantua. A street.*]
[*Enter Romeo.*]

Romeo: If I may put any faith in pleasing dreams, and rely on the truth of visions, they would seem to foretell that I am about to receive some glad tidings. My heart is joyous within me, my spirit is light and free. I feel an unusual uplifting of the soul, and happy thoughts fill my mind. In my dream, I thought that I was dead, and my beloved came to me (an odd thing that, in dreams, it is accounted no strange thing for a man to know that he is dead, and yet go on thinking!). When she found me, her caresses brought me back to life, and I recovered, feeling myself a king! Oh, if the mere dream of love gives one such rapture, how much more must the reality!

[*Enter Balthasar, dressed for riding.*]

Tidings from my native town! How fares it, Balthasar? Has Friar Laurence given you letters for me? How is my sweet wife? No ill has befallen my father, I hope? How is my beloved? That is the most important question, because all will be well if she be so.

Balthasar: Then all is well, for the lady, Juliet, is so. Her spirit now dwells in Paradise, and her mortal part is laid in the vault of the Capulets. I saw the ceremony, when she was interred at the side of her ancestors, and set out, immediately, to bring you word. Pray forgive me for being the bearer of such sad tidings, but you yourself commissioned me to carry all news to you, master.

Romeo: Can it be true? Then, fate, do your worst! You know, boy, where I live. Go there, and bring me means to write a letter, and then hire horses for our journey, for I shall leave Mantua tonight.

Balthasar: I pray you, master, be calm. Your pale cheeks and distracted gaze seem to indicate that you contemplate some desperate deed.

Romeo: Nonsense! You are quite mistaken. Go quickly and execute your task. Did Friar Laurence give you no letters for me?

Balthasar: No, master.

Romeo: It is of no importance. Go at once and procure the horses I spoke of. I will come immediately.

[*Exit Balthasar.*]

Now, my love, I will be by your side this night. I must consider how to do this. Oh, how ready is evil to fill the mind, when one is hopeless and despairing! I recollect seeing an apothecary lately gathering herbs, a man with heavy brows, clothed almost in rags. His abode is somewhere in this neighborhood. Poverty and wretchedness had worn him to the point of exhaustion, and his features were pale, thin and haggard. In his shop, which was almost bare, hung a stuffed alligator, a dead tortoise and the preserved bodies of strangely shaped fishes. Scattered here and there on the shelves were a few dry bones, some green earthen pots, bladders and old mouldy seeds, together with scraps of string, and dried heaps of rose leaves, placed widely apart, to look as though his store were greater than it is. When I saw this poverty, I thought in my heart, here is a miserable creature, who is in such dire need that if one wanted to buy a poison this man would prepare it, even though the penalty is death. That thought was an omen of my present need, and I shall buy a poison from this poor man. His house is here, as nearly as I can recollect. But, as it is a holiday, the poor wretch's shop is not open for trading. Hello! Apothecary!

[*Enter apothecary.*]

Apothecary: Who calls me with such clamor?

Romeo: I wish to speak to you. I see your poverty. Here are 40 ducats. I wish to buy a mixture of poison—one that will act so quickly, and so swiftly spread throughout the blood, that he who drinks it, being weary of his life, may instantly die, and his breath fly from his body with as instantaneous a flash as does the gunpowder, which when ignited, is hurled forth from the deadly cannon's mouth.

Apothecary: I can supply you with such a fatal potion. But the law of our city punishes with death any man who sells or circulates such poisonous drugs.

Romeo: Do you actually shrink from death? You, who are so forlorn and miserable? Hunger is written on your face, necessity and hardship show themselves in your eyes and your clothes are poor and mean. Neither the laws nor the people of the world, have ever shown you any kindness, or lent you a helping hand. No keeping of the world's laws will supply your needs, or bring you wealth. Endure poverty no longer, break the world's law, earn this money, and own the wealth I give you.

Apothecary: I will do so, but it is only my dire necessities which compel me to do it.

Romeo: This money is the price of what your poverty needs, not what your will agrees to.

Apothecary: Mix this drug with any liquid you may choose. On drinking it, the effect will be instantly fatal. It has sufficient strength to kill a score of men.

Romeo: Take this gold in return. It is a far more deadly thing, and causes the death of many more in this hateful world than any of these mixtures you are forbidden to sell. The potion you have given me is an innocent thing, in comparison with the gold I give you. Buy food with it, that you may be less lean. Adieu!

Come, gladdening drink, with me. You are no deadly poison! We will hasten to my lady's tomb together, for it is there I shall need your aid.

[*Exit.*]

ACT V · SCENE 2

[*Verona. Friar Laurence's cell.*]

[*Enter Friar John.*]

Friar John: Holy Franciscan friar! Brother, hello!

[*Enter Friar Laurence.*]

Friar Laurence: That voice should belong to Friar John. You are happily returned from Mantua! What is Romeo's reply to my letter? If he has written what he thinks, let me have the letter.

Friar John: I went first to a monastery to ask one of the brothers of our order to accompany me on my visits to the sick. While I was there, those whose duty it is to search the city to find out which houses are infected, came also, and, suspecting the presence of plague infection there, closed and sealed the gates, forbidding anyone to leave the house. The speedy journey, therefore, that I have made to Mantua was stopped at that point.

Friar Laurence: Then by whom did you send my letter to Romeo?

Friar John: I could neither forward it to Romeo, nor get anyone to carry it to you, all were so afraid of the plague. So, I here return it to you!

Friar Laurence: Oh, miserable evil fortune! By St. Francis, that letter was no unimportant, trivial thing, but bore the most weighty news, on a precious and vital subject. The greatest harm may result from its remaining undelivered to Romeo. Good brother, go at once and get me an iron bar, and bring it back here quickly.

Friar John: I will do as you ask, good Friar Laurence.

[*Exit.*]

Friar Laurence: I must go to Capulet's vault, myself! In a short time, the sweet maid will waken, and she will reproach me greatly when she hears that Romeo has never been told of all these events which have occurred since he left Verona. I must send another letter to him and, meanwhile, Juliet shall find a refuge with me, until he comes to claim her. Poor child, alive, yet dead and imprisoned in a sepulchre of the dead!

[*Exit.*]

ACT V · SCENE 3

[*A churchyard; in it, a tomb belonging to the Capulets.*]

[*Enter Paris and his page, bearing flowers and a torch.*]

Paris: Hand me the light, boy, and you go and wait over there. No, you had better extinguish the torch, for I do not wish anyone to see me. Go and lie down at full length beneath those trees, and lay your ear to the ground. As the soil of the churchyard is loose, and hollow in so many places, no one will be able to enter without your hearing their footsteps. Then whistle to me, to give me notice that someone is coming near. I will take the flowers. Now go, and do as I have directed.

Page: I feel very timid at the idea of remaining alone in this burial ground. But I will dare it!

[*Retires.*]

Paris: Fairest blossom, I here scatter blossoms on thy nuptial couch—alas, that thou should lie covered with earth and stones! And every evening, I will wet thy resting place with sweet perfumes. Or, should they fail, my tears, distilled by grief, shall water thy tomb. These shall be thy funeral rites, which I shall nightly pay. Here I will scatter fair blossoms, and mourn for thee, my love! [*The page whistles.*] That is the page's signal that someone comes. Curse the footsteps that come roaming in this direction, to interrupt the ceremonies that I would pay to my love! They bring a torch, too! Hide me for a time, friendly darkness!

[*Retires.*]

[*Enter Romeo and Balthasar, with a torch, pickaxe, etc.*]

Romeo: Give me the crowbar and the pickaxe. Wait! Here is a letter which you must take to my father, the first thing in the morning. Hand me the torch. Remember, no matter what you may see or hear, you are to remain over there and not interfere, on pain of death, with what I am about to do. The reason I wish to go down into the vault is partly that I may look on the face of my love once more. But, more still, because I wish to recover a ring which she wears, a treasured ring, which I must take from her cold hand, to employ it in a most important matter. Away, therefore, and leave me. If you should be suspicious of me, and come back to spy upon my movements, I swear that I will tear you apart, limb from limb, and scatter the fragments over this burial ground, that craves for more dead bodies to devour. This dark hour well suits my mood—both are grim and merciless, more cruel than a hungry tiger and more relentless than the raging sea.

Balthasar: I will retire at once, master. I shall not disturb you.

Romeo: You will do me a kindness by so doing. Here is money. Take it and go your way, and may you prosper. Adieu, worthy youth!

Balthasar: [*Aside.*] Regardless of all these threats, I will conceal myself near at hand. His looks fill me with dread and I suspect his intentions toward himself.

[*Retires.*]

Romeo: Thus do I wrench apart thy foul jaws, and force an entrance to thy hideous chamber, thou horrible sepulchre, whose horrid throat is filled with death, and whose gaping jaws have just devoured the sweetest delicacy in the universe—the fair and lovely Juliet! [*Opens the tomb.*] In hatred of thy gluttony, I will gorge thee with further prey!

Paris: This is the proud Montague who was exiled for the murder of Tybalt, which caused my love such sorrow that it is supposed to have cost the sweet maid her life. He has come to do some disgraceful deed upon the corpses of these two. I will seize upon him. [*Comes forward.*] You wretched Montague, cease your sacrilegious work! Will you follow up your revenge even on the dead? Convicted knave, I here arrest you. You must accompany me, without resistance. You shall die.

Romeo: In truth, I shall die. That is the reason for my presence here. Kind youth, do not urge a despairing man beyond his strength. Depart and let me be alone. Remember the corpses which lie buried here, and fear this place. I pray you, young man, do not push me into anger, and thus force me to burden myself with the crime of your death also! Oh, leave me! I swear I am more considerate to you than I am to myself, for my hand is turned against myself alone. Do not remain longer, but depart. Keep your life, I do not wish to take it. In future days, you will be able to tell how a madman allowed you, in mercy, to escape.

Paris: Your entreaties do not move me in the least, and I now arrest you as a criminal.

Romeo: You will anger me, then? You must take the consequences of your folly! Fall to!

[*They fight.*]

Page: By heaven! They are actually fighting! I must fetch the watchmen.

[*Exit.*]

Paris: Oh, you have killed me! [*Falls.*] If you have any pity, take me into the vault, and lay me by the side of Juliet.

[*Dies.*]

Romeo: By my soul, I will do it. Let me examine this youth's features. It is the young nobleman, Count Paris, who was kin to Mercutio! Did my servant not speak of him on our way here, when my mind was too agitated and my soul too shaken to pay attention to what he said? I seem to remember that he said Count Paris was to have been wedded to Juliet. Or is it only a dream, an insane fancy which my brain has conjured up because he spoke of Juliet? Thus, Paris, I take thy hand. We are kin to each other in the fellowship of misfortune! I will bury thee magnificently, but call it not a grave where thou shalt lie. Say, rather a lantern, dead youth. Is it not lit by the presence of my love, whose sweet loveliness illuminates this gloomy place until it glows like a banquet hall of kings? Lie there, dead youth, buried by one who is now to die also!

[*Laying Paris in the tomb.*]

It often happens that men's spirits are more cheerful just before they die, than they have been for some time. Their attendants call this a lightening before death. It seems to me that I may term this interlude before my death, the same! O, my beloved, my dear wife! Though death has stolen away thy breath, and drunk its sweetness, his might has not yet triumphed over thy loveliness that still does not admit defeat. Its rose-hued banner is still displayed in thy lips and cheeks, and death's pale colors are not yet flying there. Thou too, Tybalt, are laid to rest here, in thy gory shroud. How can I better make amends to thee for cutting short thy young life, than by killing thy former foe?

Kinsman, I ask thy pardon. Ah, my beloved, why is thy beauty still so entrancing? Must I think that death, as though it were a real person, can feel affection, and that the pinched and haggard ghost holds thee in this gloomy place to be the object of his hateful love? To guard thee from that, I will not leave thee again, but in this place of shadows I will remain forever, with my earthly attendants. Here will I make my last long habitation, and free my earth-worn body, spent and exhausted with the woes of this life, from the burden of bearing any longer the sorrows of a disastrous fate. Take your last glance, eyes; and arms, give your last caress; and lips, the portals of the breath, impress your seal, with a pure and holy kiss, upon an everlasting agreement with hungry death! Hurry, thou harsh conductor, thou distasteful leader, thou reckless steersman, now quickly bear this storm-tossed vessel to its final shipwreck! Juliet, I drink to thee! [*Drinks.*] O apothecary, thou hast kept thy word. The potion certainly acts swiftly! With this last kiss, beloved, my life is gone!

[*Dies.*]

[*Enter, at the other end of the churchyard,
Friar Laurence with a lantern, crowbar and spade.*]

Friar Laurence: May St. Francis be my aid! My aged limbs have carried me stumblingly tonight among the graves. Who's there?

Balthasar: A friend is here. One who is well acquainted with you.

Friar Laurence: My blessing upon thee! My dear fellow, what torch is that I see, uselessly burning amid worms and dead men's bones? It appears to be burning in the vault of the Capulets.

Balthasar: It is burning there, good father. Within the vault is your esteemed friend, my master.

Friar Laurence: Whom do you mean?

Balthasar: Why, Romeo.

Friar Laurence: When did he enter?

Balthasar: A good half-hour ago.

Friar Laurence: Come with me to the tomb.

Balthasar: I cannot venture to do that, sir, because my master, Romeo, thinks that I have left this place long ago. He forbade me, with terrible threats, to remain and watch his movements.

Friar Laurence: Rest here, then, and I will go by myself. My heart is filled with dread. I am greatly afraid some terrible misfortune has happened!

Balthasar: It seemed to me, as I rested beneath these boughs, that I saw a vision of Romeo and another in deadly combat, and my master killed his foe.

Friar Laurence: Romeo! [*Advances.*] Alas! Alas! How came these bloodstains upon the stones at the mouth of the vault? What do these ownerless and bloodstained weapons forebode, lying here by this still and solemn sepulchre? [*Enters the tomb.*] Romeo! White and wan! And another! Oh! Paris also, drenched in gore! What dire misfortune has taken place in this unlucky hour? See! The maiden wakes!

[*Juliet awakes.*]

Juliet: O good father, how your presence comforts me! Where is my husband! I recollect where you said I should wake, and I am there, I see. Where is my love?

[*Noise within.*]

Friar Laurence: What sounds are those I hear? Dear maiden, let us leave this den of death, foul odors and strange slumber. Our plans have all been overthrown by a mightier Power than we poor mortals can contend against. Come, leave this place, your beloved husband lies there dead. Paris, also, is gone. Come with me, and I will arrange for some good nuns to shelter you. Come at once, for the watchmen are almost here. Pray, dear Juliet, hasten, and go with me. [*Noise again.*] I must not remain a moment longer!

Juliet: Then go. Depart; I shall remain here.

[*Exit Friar Laurence.*]

What is this? My dear husband's fingers are clasping a cup. I see that his untimely death was brought about by poison. Ah, knave, have thou drained it dry, nor left one kindly drop to aid thy love to follow thee! If I kiss thee on the mouth, perhaps some of the fatal drink may yet remain there, to restore me to thee in death! [*Kisses him.*] His lips are not yet cold!

First Watchman: [*Within.*] Go before, boy, and show me the way.

Juliet: Do I hear someone coming? Then I will act swiftly. O fortunate chance! Here is a weapon! [*Snatching Romeo's dagger.*] Thus, I sheathe it in my bosom. [*Stabs herself.*] There remain, and let me take leave of life!

[*Dies.*]

[*Enter watchman with page of Paris.*]

Page: It was there, where you see the light burning, that I left them.

First Watchman: There are marks of blood on the ground. Look carefully around the churchyard, some of you, and if you meet with any persons near, arrest them. [*Exit some.*] A piteous spectacle! Count Paris lying dead, and the lady, Juliet, scarcely cold, and blood still flowing from her wound, although she was buried here, for dead, two days ago! Go, some of you, and take the news of this to the prince, and also arouse the Montagues and Capulets. Others, help to look for the offenders in this affair. [*Exit other watchmen.*] The ground on which these unhappy beings lie is plainly before us, but the cause or ground of this calamity we cannot know until we have further details.

[*Re-enter some of the watchmen, with Balthasar.*]

Second Watchman: This is Romeo's servant, whom we discovered in the churchyard.

First Watchman: Guard him carefully until the prince arrives.

[*Re-enter other watchmen, with Friar Laurence.*]

Third Watchman: We found this friar sighing, trembling and weeping as he was leaving the churchyard, and we took these tools from him and brought him here.

First Watchman: This looks most suspicious. Keep the friar safely also.

[*Enter the prince and attendants.*]

Prince: What disaster has happened, at such an early hour, that we have been disturbed from our repose so soon?

[*Enter Capulet, Lady Capulet, and others.*]

Capulet: What can have happened, that the people outdoors make such a clamor?

Lady Capulet: The citizens all seem to be hurrying toward our vault, with confused cries of "Romeo," "Juliet" and "Paris."

Prince: What new dread is this, which is bursting upon us?

First Watchman: Count Paris has been killed, prince, and Romeo lies dead here also. While Juliet, whom all supposed dead some time ago, is newly slain, and her body not yet cold.

Prince: Search, search most carefully, and find out how this villainous crime has happened.

First Watchman: We have already taken the servant of dead Romeo, and this friar, and we found, in their possession, such tools as would enable one to force open the entrance to the vault.

Capulet: Oh, Heaven! See, wife, the blood flowing from Juliet's wounds! What an error has this weapon committed! Its sheath on Romeo's belt is hanging empty, while the dagger has, mistakenly, found a home in the heart of Juliet!

Lady Capulet: Alas! This death-strewn vault, like the tolling of a knell, counsels me to prepare for my own end.

[*Enter Montague and others.*]

Prince: Approach, Montague. You have been summoned here early, but death has been here before you, and has already vanquished your son, Romeo.

Montague: Alas! My sovereign prince, my wife has died this night, of sorrow at the banishment of Romeo. What new calamity is now about to overwhelm an aged man?

Prince: The answer is before you!

Montague: Unmannerly boy! This is no civil behavior to

outdistance thy father and reach the tomb so long before him!

Prince: Cease these wild outcries for a time, until we can understand clearly what has happened, and can find out from the confused account of these events, the cause and origin of these misfortunes. Then, I will take the lead in your grievances, and will see that justice is done, under any circumstances. Until then, be calm. Cease your lamentations and wait with patience for the true account of the matter. Bring the suspected persons before me.

Friar Laurence: Suspicion lies heaviest upon me. Though I am less able than others to commit the deed, yet the circumstances under which I come before you, both as to time and place, tell greatly against me. I stand here now, both to accuse myself of what I really did, and to clear myself of the suspicion which rests upon me.

Prince: Then tell us, without delay, all that you know of this affair.

Friar Laurence: I will tell my story quickly, for the time which yet remains to me of life is not long enough to drag out a wearisome tale. Romeo, who lies dead before your eyes, was wedded to Juliet, and she, who lies by his side, was his true and loyal wife. They were married by me. The day on which they were secretly wed was the day on which Tybalt met his premature death. For this, the newly wedded Romeo was exiled from Verona, and Juliet's tears were on his account, and not on account of her cousin's death. Then, in order to free her, as they thought, from this attack of sorrow, her parents engaged her to the young count, and fixed her marriage day in spite of her opposition. At this, she came to my cell in great distress and despair, and begged me to contrive some scheme whereby she might avoid being married a second time, failing which, she vowed she would kill herself, then and there.

I, by my learning, was able to make up a sleeping potion for her, which had the effect of giving her all the appearance of death. When she had gone, I wrote to her husband, telling him all this, and arranging that he should come to Verona on this very night, and be with me when I rescued her from her temporary tomb. For about this time, the effect of the sleeping potion would wear off. But my letter never reached Romeo. The man to whom I entrusted it was detained unexpectedly in Verona, and I received my letter back again last night. I then set forth to come to the vault alone, at the hour at which I had calculated Juliet would wake and, on taking her from the tomb, I meant to convey her to my cell, where she could have remained, in secret, until an opportunity came to send a letter again to Romeo. I arrived at this place a few moments before she woke. But, on my arrival, I discovered that all too soon had death been here before me, and the young count, with faithful Romeo, already lay here dead.

Just then the lady awoke, and I begged of her that she would accompany me, and leave this place, and try to endure this trial with resignation. The noise of people approaching made me leave the tomb in fear, but Juliet, distracted with grief, refused to come away. She remained behind, and I now see that she took her own life, after my departure. This is the true account of these events. Her nurse knew of them, also, as far as the marriage is concerned. If you think that any part of these calamities happened through neglect of mine, or that my actions have hastened the catastrophe, I am willing to be deprived of what remains to me of life, or to be punished according to the sternest measures of the law.

Prince: We have never yet had reason to doubt your goodness. Bring forward Romeo's servant, and let us hear what he knows of the matter.

Balthasar: I carried the tidings of Juliet's death to my master in Mantua, and he immediately rode here to Verona, and came straight to this tomb. Then he gave me this letter, which he ordered me to deliver to his father first thing in the morning. When he entered the sepulchre, he threatened to slay me unless I went away and left him undisturbed.

Prince: Let me see the letter he gave you. Where is Count Paris's page, who summoned the watchmen? What was your master doing in the churchyard, young man?

Page: He came to scatter flowers on the tomb of his love, and he commanded me to remain at a distance while he did so. I obeyed him. Presently, someone came, bringing a torch, and began to force open the vault. In a few minutes, my master drew his sword, and they fought. Then, I hurried off to bring the watchmen.

Prince: The friar's story is fully borne out by this letter. It tells of the progress of their affection, and of the news of her death. Romeo has written that he came here intending to die by Juliet's side, by means of a poison which he purchased from a poor apothecary in Mantua. Where are these foes? Look, both of you, and see the terrible destruction that your hatred has caused, and the terrible penalty heaven has exacted. Your dearest ones lie dead of love, because of your hate, while I, myself, have lost two of my kin, in consequence of having been too lenient with you on the subject of your quarrels. Thus punishment is portioned out to all!

Capulet: Give me your hand in friendship, Montague. The marriage of my daughter has brought me this, a sufficient gift on her wedding with your son. No greater gift could I ask.

Montague: But a greater one I will give: I will erect a statue of pure gold to the memory of your daughter. There shall be no such rare and valuable statue as hers, as long as this city is known as Verona.

Capulet: And Romeo's, by her side, shall be as costly, yet how meagre and insufficient the atonement, for the woes our hatred has made!

Prince: A clouded joy is ours, this morning, at this reconciliation. Even the sun, day's joyous lord, seems to hide his face in grief. Let all depart, and these sorrowful events can be discussed at greater length. Some of those who have taken part in them must be punished, but others will be set free. Never yet did any hear a sadder tale than the story of these two unhappy lovers!

[*Exit.*]